SALZBURG

TRAVEL GUIDE 2024-2025

ALL RIGHTS RESERVED.

No part of this publication may be reproduced, distributed, or transmitted in any form or by any means, including photocopying, recording, or other electronic or mechanical methods, without the prior written permission of the publisher, except in the case of brief quotations embodied in critical reviews and certain other noncommercial uses permitted by copyright law.

DISCLAIMER

This travel guide is provided for informational purposes only. The information contained herein is believed to be accurate and reliable as of the publication date, but may be subject to change. We are not making any warranty, express or implied, with respect to the content of this guide.

Users of this guide are responsible for verifying information independently and consulting appropriate authorities and resources prior to travel. We are not liable for any loss or damage caused by the reliance on information contained in this guide.

Information regarding travel advisories, visas, health, safety, and other important considerations can change rapidly. Users are advised to check for the most up-to-date information from official government and travel industry sources before embarking on any trip.

Travel inherently involves risk, and users are responsible for making their own informed decisions and accepting any associated risks.

TABLE OF CONTENTS

1. Introduction to Salzburg..5
   1.1 Overview of Salzburg..5
   1.2 Brief History..7
   1.3 Culture and Traditions..8

2. Getting There and Around..10
   2.1 Transportation Options..10
   2.2 Navigating the City..13
   2.3 Tips for Getting Around..15

Top Attractions..18
   3.1 Hohensalzburg Fortress..18
   3.2 Mirabell Palace and Gardens..22
   3.3 Mozart's Birthplace..28
   3.4 Salzburg Cathedral..32
   3.5 Sound of Music Tour Highlights..36

Local Cuisine..42
   4.1 Traditional Dishes to Try..42
   4.2 Best Restaurants and Cafés..45
   4.3 Food Markets and Street Food..50

Accommodation
   5.1 Recommended Hotels and Hostels..53
   5.2 Unique Stays (e.g., Boutique Hotels)..56
   5.3 Tips for Booking..64

Seasonal Events and Festivals..67
   6.1 Overview of Annual Festivals..67
   6.2 Winter Holiday Celebrations..69
   6.3 Summer Events and Outdoor Activities..72

Day Trips and Excursions..76
   7.1 Exploring the Surrounding Region..76
   7.2 Popular Day Trip Destinations..79
   7.3 Nature and Outdoor Activities..82

Travel Tips and Practical Information..88
   8.1 Language and Communication..88
   8.2 Currency and Payments..93
   8.3 Safety Tips and Emergency Contacts..96
   8.4 Local Customs and Etiquette..100
   Acknowledgments..107

1. Introduction to Salzburg

1.1 Overview of Salzburg

Salzburg is a beautiful city in Austria, known for its stunning landscapes, rich history, and vibrant culture. Nestled between the Alps and the Salzach River, it offers a mix of natural beauty and charming architecture. Salzburg is often called the "Rome of the North" because of its impressive baroque buildings and historical significance.

The city is famous for being the birthplace of Wolfgang Amadeus Mozart, one of the greatest composers in history. His influence is felt throughout the city, with numerous monuments and events celebrating his legacy. Visitors can explore his childhood home and enjoy concerts featuring his music, making Salzburg a must-visit for music lovers.

Salzburg is also known for its well-preserved medieval and baroque architecture. The Hohensalzburg Fortress towers over the city, providing breathtaking views of the surroundings. The fortress dates back to the 11th century and is one of the largest medieval castles in Europe. Exploring its grounds allows visitors to step back in time and appreciate the city's rich heritage.

Another highlight is the Mirabell Palace, famous for its beautiful gardens and fountains. The palace was built in the early 18th century and is a UNESCO World Heritage Site. The gardens are a popular spot for both locals and tourists, offering a perfect place to relax and take photos.

Salzburg's charming old town (Altstadt) is a UNESCO World Heritage Site filled with narrow streets, quaint shops, and cozy cafés. Here, you can find the famous Getreidegasse, a bustling street lined with shops selling everything from traditional Austrian crafts to delicious pastries. The vibrant atmosphere of the old town is perfect for leisurely strolls, allowing visitors to soak in the city's charm.

Throughout the year, Salzburg hosts various cultural events and festivals, such as the Salzburg Festival, which attracts artists and audiences from around the world. This festival celebrates classical music, opera, and theater, showcasing top talent and offering unforgettable performances.

In summary, Salzburg is a city that captivates visitors with its rich history, stunning architecture, and vibrant culture. Whether you're exploring the historic sites, enjoying a concert, or savoring local cuisine, Salzburg offers a unique and memorable experience for everyone.

1.2 Brief History

Salzburg has a fascinating history that dates back over a thousand years. Its name, which means "Salt Fortress," reflects its origins as a center for salt mining. Salt was a valuable resource in ancient times, and its trade helped the city thrive.

The area was first settled by the Celts around 500 BC. Later, the Romans arrived in 15 BC and established a settlement called *Juvavum*, which became an important military outpost. The Romans built roads, homes, and public buildings, laying the foundation for Salzburg's future development.

After the fall of the Roman Empire, Salzburg became part of the territory controlled by various Germanic tribes. By the 8th century, it was under the influence of the Christian church. In 696 AD, Saint Rupert, a Benedictine monk, founded the Abbey of St. Peter and became the city's first bishop. His efforts to spread Christianity laid the groundwork for Salzburg's religious importance.

During the Middle Ages, Salzburg became a significant ecclesiastical principality, ruled by the archbishops. They held both religious and political power, making the city a center of church affairs. The archbishops were responsible for building many of the city's most famous landmarks, including the impressive Hohensalzburg Fortress, which began construction in 1077.

In the 17th and 18th centuries, Salzburg flourished as a cultural hub. The city became renowned for its art, music, and architecture. It was during this period that Wolfgang Amadeus Mozart was born in 1756. His musical genius would go on to put Salzburg on the map as a center for classical music.

However, the city faced challenges in the 19th century. In 1805, Salzburg was annexed by Bavaria and later became part of Austria in 1816. Despite these political changes, Salzburg maintained its cultural significance.

In the 20th century, Salzburg continued to grow and develop, especially after World War II. The Salzburg Festival, founded in 1920, became an internationally acclaimed event, showcasing the city's dedication to music and arts.

Today, Salzburg is a thriving city that attracts millions of visitors each year. Its rich history is evident in its architecture, cultural events, and vibrant atmosphere. The blend of ancient and modern influences makes Salzburg a unique destination where the past and present coexist harmoniously.

1.3 Culture and Traditions

Salzburg boasts a rich cultural heritage shaped by its history, geography, and prominent figures, especially Wolfgang Amadeus Mozart. The city is a vibrant blend of traditional and contemporary influences, making it a fascinating destination for visitors.

1. Musical Heritage

Salzburg is famously known as the birthplace of Mozart, and music is a vital part of the city's identity. The annual **Salzburg Festival**, held every summer, is a highlight, attracting artists and audiences from around the globe. This festival features opera, classical music concerts, and theatrical performances, celebrating both Mozart's works and other classical compositions. Throughout the year, you can find numerous concerts, chamber music events, and performances in venues such as the **Mozarteum** and the **Great Festival Hall**.

2. Traditional Arts and Crafts

The city is home to various traditional crafts, including ceramics, glassmaking, and textile production. Many local artisans continue to practice these skills, creating unique handcrafted items that reflect Salzburg's artistic heritage. Visitors can explore shops and markets in the old town to find beautiful souvenirs, such as traditional Salzburg hats, handmade ornaments, and pottery.

3. Festivals and Celebrations

Salzburg hosts a variety of festivals throughout the year, celebrating everything from music and art to local traditions. Besides the Salzburg Festival, notable events include the **Advent Markets** during the Christmas season, where visitors can enjoy festive decorations, crafts, and traditional foods like roasted chestnuts . The **Salzburg Easter Festival** is another significant event, featuring classical music concerts and performances in beautiful historic venues.

4. Gastronomy

Salzburg's culinary scene is a reflection of its cultural diversity. Traditional dishes include **Mozartkugel** (chocolate-covered marzipan balls), **Schnitzel**, and **Salzburger Nockerl**, a sweet soufflé that is a local specialty. Many restaurants offer authentic Austrian cuisine, often with a modern twist. Exploring the local food markets, like the **Getreidegasse Market**, allows visitors to taste fresh produce, cheeses, and meats while experiencing the vibrant atmosphere.

5. Religious Traditions

The city has a strong religious heritage, primarily due to its history as a center for Christianity. The **Archbishopric of Salzburg** played a significant role in the development of the city. Visitors can explore beautiful churches, such as the **Salzburg Cathedral**, known for its stunning baroque architecture. Religious festivals and celebrations, like **Easter** and **Christmas**, are important events in the local culture, featuring processions, special services, and traditional music.

6. Connection to Nature

Salzburg's stunning natural surroundings also influence its culture. The nearby **Alps** offer opportunities for outdoor activities, such as hiking, skiing, and snowboarding. Local traditions often celebrate the region's natural beauty, with festivals that highlight the importance of agriculture, such as the **Harvest Festival**. This connection to nature is evident in the city's many parks and gardens, which provide peaceful spaces for relaxation and recreation.

In summary, Salzburg's culture and traditions are a rich tapestry woven from its historical significance, artistic legacy, and natural beauty. The city celebrates its past while embracing modern influences, making it a vibrant destination that offers something for everyone. Whether through music, art, food, or local customs, visitors to Salzburg can experience a unique and enchanting culture that leaves a lasting impression.

2. Getting There and Around

2.1 Transportation Options

Getting to Salzburg and moving around the city is convenient, thanks to its well-developed transportation system. Whether you are arriving by plane, train, or car, there are plenty of options to help you start your journey in this beautiful city.

1. Arriving by Plane

Salzburg has its own airport, **Salzburg Airport W. A. Mozart (SZG)**, located just a few kilometers from the city center. It's a small but modern airport with flights connecting to major cities across Europe. Upon arriving at the airport, you have several options to reach the city:

- **Bus**: The airport bus runs regularly between the airport and the city center. The journey takes about 20 minutes and is affordable. Look for the **Line 2 bus** that goes to the central bus station (Wiener Neustädter Straße), where you can easily connect to other parts of the city.
- **Taxi**: Taxis are available outside the terminal. A taxi ride to the city center takes around 15 minutes, depending on traffic. This option is more expensive but offers door-to-door service.
- **Rental Cars**: If you prefer to drive, several car rental companies operate at the airport. Renting a car gives you the flexibility to explore the surrounding regions and beautiful landscapes at your own pace.

2. Arriving by Train

Salzburg is well connected to Austria and other European cities by train. The main train station, **Salzburg Hauptbahnhof (Hbf)**, is located just a short walk from the city center. Here are some tips for traveling by train:

- **From Vienna**: Trains from Vienna to Salzburg run frequently and take about 2.5 hours. The scenery along the way is beautiful, making it a pleasant journey.

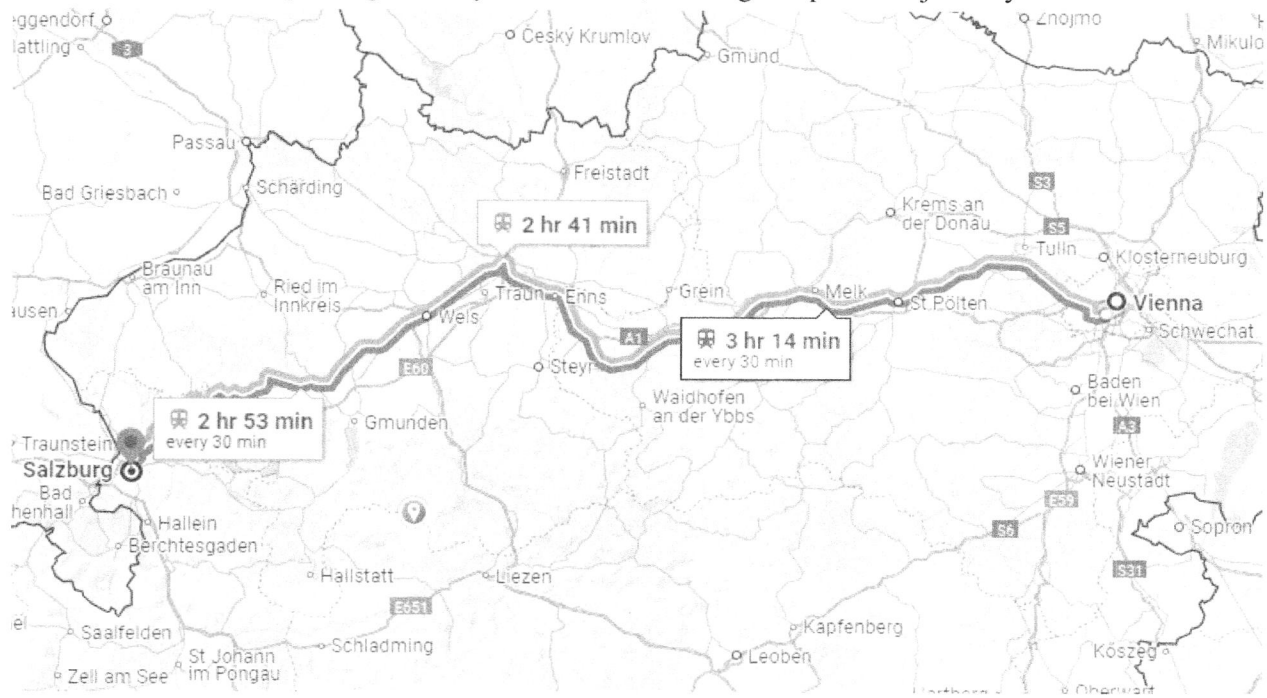

VIENNA TO SALZBURG BY TRAIN

- **From Munich**: Trains from Munich take about 1.5 to 2 hours, and there are several departures each day. This is a popular route for visitors coming from Germany.

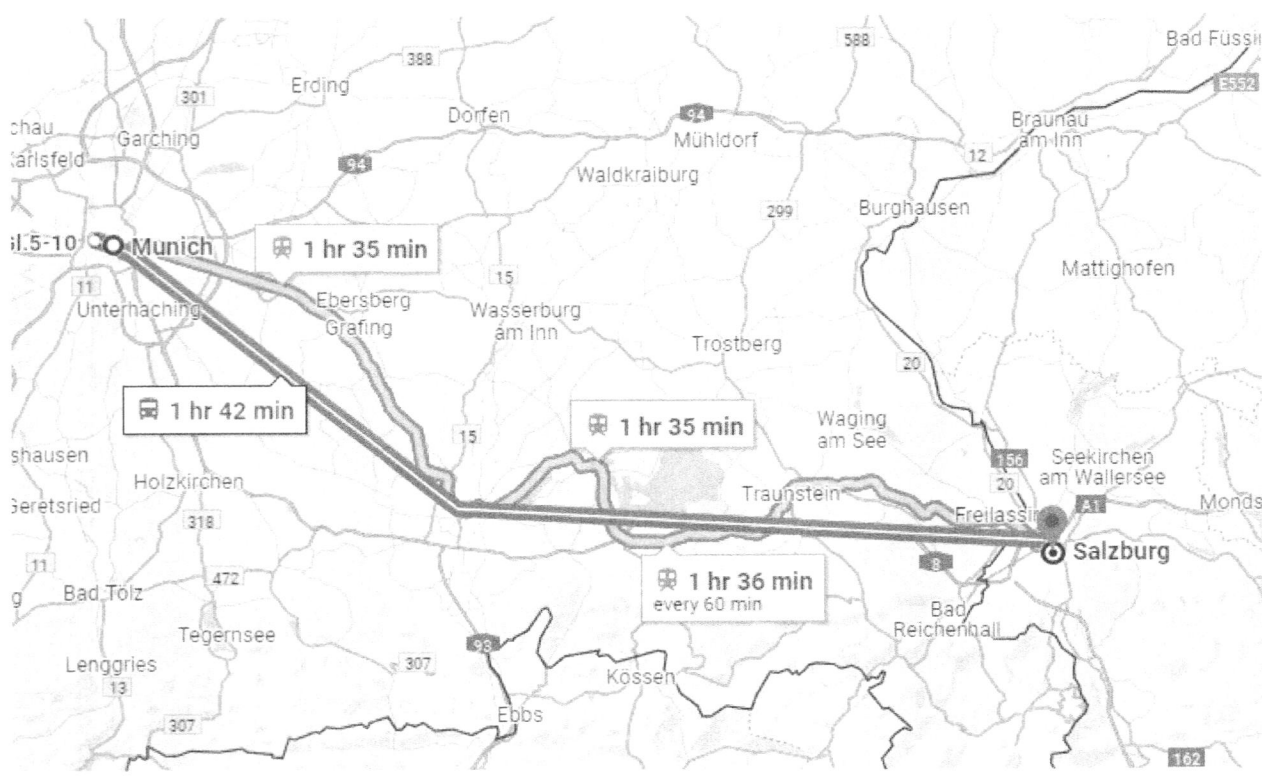

FROM MUNICH TO SALZBURG BY TRAIN

- **Local Transport**: Once you arrive at Salzburg Hbf, you can easily reach your accommodation or the city center. There are buses and taxis available outside the station, or you can walk to the city center in about 20 minutes.

3. Arriving by Car

If you prefer to drive, Salzburg is accessible via major highways. The **A1 motorway** connects Salzburg to Vienna and Linz, while the **A8 motorway** links it to Munich. Here are some things to keep in mind when driving:

- **Parking**: While driving in the city, finding parking can be challenging, especially in the old town. Look for parking garages or designated parking areas. Some popular parking garages include **Altstadt Garage** and **Müllner Brücke Garage**. It's best to park your car and explore the city on foot.
- **Traffic Rules**: Be aware of local traffic rules, such as speed limits and parking regulations. Austria has strict laws regarding drink driving, so it's essential to adhere to these rules for your safety.

4. Getting Around the City

Once you are in Salzburg, the city offers various options for getting around:

- **Public Transport**: Salzburg has an efficient public transportation system that includes buses and trams. The **Salzburg AG** operates most of these services. You can buy single tickets or day passes, which are valid on all buses and trams. The buses run frequently, making it easy to reach popular attractions.
- **Walking**: The best way to explore Salzburg's charming old town is on foot. Many attractions, such as the Mirabell Palace and Hohensalzburg Fortress, are within walking distance of each other. Walking allows you to discover hidden gems, quaint shops, and cozy cafés along the way.
- **Bicycles**: Cycling is a popular way to explore Salzburg, especially during the warmer months. You can rent bicycles from various shops around the city. There are dedicated bike lanes, and riding along the banks of the Salzach River offers beautiful views.
- **Taxis and Ride-Sharing**: Taxis are readily available throughout the city. They can be hailed on the street or booked via phone. Ride-sharing services like **Uber** are also available in Salzburg, providing an alternative way to get around.

In conclusion, getting to and around Salzburg is easy and convenient, with a variety of transportation options available. Whether you arrive by plane, train, or car, you will find that the city's public transport, walking paths, and bicycle routes make it simple to explore all the beauty and charm that Salzburg has to offer.

2.2 Navigating the City

Navigating Salzburg is straightforward, thanks to its compact size and well-organized layout. With its charming old town, picturesque streets, and efficient public transportation, you can easily find your way around and explore the many attractions this beautiful city has to offer. Here are some tips to help you navigate Salzburg:

1. Maps and Navigation Apps

- **Physical Maps**: Upon arrival, you can pick up a free city map at tourist information centers, hotels, or the airport. These maps highlight key attractions, public transport routes, and walking paths, making it easy to plan your day.

- **Mobile Apps**: Download navigation apps like **Google Maps** or **Citymapper** to help you find directions, public transport routes, and estimated travel times. Many apps also work offline, allowing you to navigate without using mobile data.

2. Understanding the Layout

- **Old Town (Altstadt)**: The heart of Salzburg is its historic old town, which is a UNESCO World Heritage Site. The old town is easy to navigate on foot, with narrow streets and squares filled with shops, cafés, and historic buildings. Key landmarks, such as **Mozart's Birthplace**, **Salzburg Cathedral**, and **Mirabell Palace**, are all within walking distance of each other.
- **Main Streets**: The two main streets in the old town are **Getreidegasse** and **Griesgasse**. Getreidegasse is famous for its shops and traditional storefronts, while Griesgasse leads towards the river and the iconic views of Hohensalzburg Fortress.
- **Landmarks as Navigation Aids**: Use prominent landmarks to orient yourself. For example, Hohensalzburg Fortress, which sits atop the hill, is visible from many parts of the city and can help you determine your location. The Salzach River also serves as a good reference point, running through the city.

3. Public Transportation Routes

- **Buses and Trams**: Salzburg's public transportation system is reliable and covers most areas of the city. Buses and trams are marked with route numbers and destinations, making it easy to find your way. The main bus terminal is located at **Hauptbahnhof (Hbf)**, where multiple lines converge, allowing for easy transfers.
- **Stops and Schedules**: Bus stops are clearly marked with route numbers and information on when the next bus will arrive. Most stops have schedules displayed, indicating departure times for the day. Buses typically run every 10-15 minutes during peak hours, making it convenient to catch one without long waits.

4. Accessibility

- **Pedestrian-Friendly**: Salzburg is a very walkable city, especially in the old town, where many streets are pedestrian-only. Take your time to stroll through the charming streets, enjoy the beautiful architecture, and discover hidden squares and gardens.
- **Public Transport Accessibility**: Public transportation in Salzburg is also designed to accommodate people with mobility issues. Most buses and trams have low floors for easy boarding, and some stations offer elevators and ramps.

5. Guided Tours

- **Walking Tours**: Consider joining a guided walking tour to learn more about Salzburg's history and culture. These tours typically cover major landmarks and provide valuable insights from knowledgeable guides. They are a great way to get your bearings and discover interesting facts about the city.
- **Bike Tours**: If you prefer cycling, look for bike tours that guide you through the city and its surrounding areas. This can be a fun and active way to explore, especially along the scenic river paths.

6. Local Tips

- **Watch for Signs**: Look for street signs that indicate directions to popular attractions. These signs often include maps or directional arrows that make it easier to navigate.
- **Ask Locals for Help**: If you're unsure about directions or need assistance, don't hesitate to ask locals. Salzburg residents are generally friendly and willing to help visitors find their way.

In summary, navigating Salzburg is easy and enjoyable. With its walkable old town, reliable public transportation, and helpful resources, you'll have no trouble exploring this enchanting city. Take your time, soak in the sights, and enjoy the journey as you discover all that Salzburg has to offer.

2.3 Tips for Getting Around

Getting around Salzburg can be a delightful experience, thanks to its compact layout and efficient transportation options. Here are some practical tips to help you navigate the city smoothly and enjoy your time exploring all that Salzburg has to offer.

1. Plan Your Routes

- **Research Ahead**: Before you head out, take a few minutes to plan your route to your desired destination. Check the distance between attractions and whether walking or public transport is more suitable. Having a general idea of where you're going can save you time and help you make the most of your day.
- **Use Maps**: Familiarize yourself with a city map or a navigation app. Highlight the key attractions you want to visit and the best routes to take. Knowing the main streets and landmarks will make it easier to find your way around.

2. Purchase Transportation Passes

- **Public Transport Passes**: If you plan to use public transport frequently, consider purchasing a day pass or multi-day pass. These passes provide unlimited travel on buses and trams within the city for a set price, making it convenient and cost-effective.
- **Combination Tickets**: Some tickets combine public transport with entrance to popular attractions, which can save you both time and money. Check for these options when planning your visits.

3. Timing is Key

- **Avoid Peak Hours**: If possible, try to avoid using public transport during peak hours (typically 7:30 AM to 9:00 AM and 4:30 PM to 6:00 PM). Buses and trams can get crowded, making your journey less comfortable. Traveling during off-peak times can provide a more pleasant experience.
- **Check Schedules**: Be aware of public transport schedules, especially on weekends and holidays when services may run less frequently. Knowing when the last bus or tram leaves can help you avoid being stranded.

4. Dress Comfortably for Walking

- **Wear Comfortable Shoes**: Since Salzburg is a walkable city, be prepared to do a lot of walking. Comfortable shoes are essential, especially when exploring the cobblestone streets of the old town. This will ensure you can enjoy your time without discomfort.
- **Dress for the Weather**: Check the weather forecast before heading out. Dress in layers, especially in the cooler months, and be prepared for sudden changes in weather. An umbrella or a light jacket can come in handy if rain is expected.

5. Stay Aware of Your Surroundings

- **Be Mindful of Traffic**: While walking or biking, always stay alert and be aware of your surroundings. Watch for trams and buses, especially at crossings, and follow pedestrian signals.
- **Keep Valuables Secure**: Like in any city, be mindful of your belongings. Keep bags close to you and avoid displaying valuables. Using a money belt or a secure bag can help you keep your essentials safe.

6. Utilize Tourist Information Centers

- **Visit Tourist Centers**: Make a stop at one of the local tourist information centers. They can provide helpful maps, brochures, and advice on public transport. Staff members are usually knowledgeable about the city and can answer your questions about getting around.

- **Ask for Recommendations**: Don't hesitate to ask for local recommendations on the best ways to reach your destinations or for tips on hidden gems in the city.

7. Be Open to Different Modes of Transport

- **Bicycles**: If you're feeling adventurous, consider renting a bicycle. There are many bike rental shops, and cycling can be a fun way to explore the city and its surrounding areas. Look for dedicated bike paths, especially along the river.
- **Taxis and Ride-Sharing**: If you're in a hurry or prefer a more comfortable option, taxis and ride-sharing services like Uber are available in Salzburg. While they can be more expensive, they offer a quick way to get to your destination.

8. Enjoy the Journey

- **Take Your Time**: Don't rush through your visits. Allow yourself to explore, take photos, and appreciate the beautiful surroundings. Sometimes the journey can be just as enjoyable as the destination itself.
- **Experience Local Culture**: While getting around, take the opportunity to stop at cafés, shops, or local markets. Engaging with the local culture will enhance your experience and give you a deeper appreciation of Salzburg.

In summary, getting around Salzburg is straightforward and enjoyable, with a little planning and awareness. By using public transportation, walking, and exploring the city at your own pace, you can fully immerse yourself in the charm and beauty of Salzburg while making the most of your visit.

Top Attractions

3.1 Hohensalzburg Fortress

Overview

Hohensalzburg Fortress, known as *Festung Hohensalzburg* in German, is one of Salzburg's most iconic landmarks and a must-visit attraction for anyone traveling to the city. Perched on a hilltop, this impressive fortress offers stunning views of Salzburg and the surrounding Alps, making it a perfect spot for photography and sightseeing.

History

The fortress has a rich history dating back to its construction in 1077, initiated by Archbishop Gebhard von Helfenstein. It was built to serve as a stronghold and a residence for the archbishops of Salzburg. Over the centuries, the fortress was expanded and fortified, reflecting the architectural styles of different periods. It has never been conquered, which speaks to its impressive design and strategic location.

During the Middle Ages, Hohensalzburg played a vital role in protecting the city and its inhabitants from invasions and conflicts. It served not only as a military stronghold but also as a center for governance and administration. Today, the fortress stands as a symbol of Salzburg's historical and cultural heritage.

Getting There

- **By Foot:** If you enjoy walking, you can reach the fortress from the old town by taking the scenic Festungsberg, a well-marked trail that leads you uphill through beautiful gardens and forested paths. The walk takes about 30 minutes and offers lovely views along the way.
- **Funicular Railway:** For a more comfortable ascent, you can take the Hohensalzburg Funicular, which departs from the base of the fortress near the old town. The ride only

takes about 5 minutes and provides stunning views as you ascend. The funicular operates throughout the day, and tickets can be purchased at the station.

Exploring the Fortress

Once you arrive at Hohensalzburg Fortress, there is plenty to see and do:

1. **Museums:** The fortress houses several interesting museums that showcase its history and the culture of Salzburg. Highlights include:
   - **The Fortress Museum:** This museum provides insights into the fortress's history, featuring exhibits on its construction, life in the fortress, and its role in the region's military history.
   - **Marionette Museum:** This unique museum showcases the art of marionette puppetry, with beautiful handcrafted puppets and performances that delight visitors of all ages.
2. **The Great Hall:** One of the fortress's most impressive spaces is the Great Hall (*Großer Saal*), which features stunning wooden beams and intricate decorations. The hall is often used for concerts and events, and its acoustics are exceptional.
3. **St. George's Chapel:** This charming chapel is located within the fortress and is worth a visit. It features beautiful stained glass windows and an elegant altar. The chapel reflects the spiritual life of the archbishops and is still used for religious ceremonies today.
4. **The Fortress Walls:** Walk along the fortress walls to enjoy breathtaking panoramic views of Salzburg, the Salzach River, and the surrounding mountains. There are several viewpoints along the way where you can take photos and appreciate the scenery.
5. **Courtyards and Gardens:** Explore the lovely courtyards and gardens within the fortress grounds. These areas are perfect for a leisurely stroll and provide a glimpse into the everyday life of those who lived and worked in the fortress.

Dining and Souvenirs

- **Dining:** If you get hungry during your visit, the fortress has a café and restaurant where you can enjoy a meal or a snack while taking in the beautiful views. Outdoor seating allows you to relax in the fresh air, making it a lovely spot to recharge before continuing your exploration.
- **Souvenir Shop:** Don't forget to stop by the fortress's gift shop, where you can find unique souvenirs, including local crafts, books, and traditional Austrian treats. These make great keepsakes or gifts for loved ones.

Visitor Information

- **Opening Hours:** Hohensalzburg Fortress is open year-round, but hours may vary depending on the season. It's best to check the official website for current opening times and any special events or closures.
- **Tickets:** Tickets can be purchased at the entrance or online. Prices may vary for adults, children, and families. Combo tickets that include the funicular ride and museum entries are often available, providing good value for visitors.
- **Accessibility:** The fortress is accessible by funicular, making it suitable for visitors with mobility challenges. However, some areas may be steep or uneven, so plan accordingly.

Tips for Your Visit

- **Best Time to Visit:** For the best experience, try to visit during the morning or late afternoon when the crowds are smaller. Early mornings also provide a chance to see the city bathed in the golden light of sunrise.
- **Guided Tours:** Consider joining a guided tour for a deeper understanding of the fortress's history and significance. Knowledgeable guides can provide fascinating stories and insights that you might not learn otherwise.

In summary, Hohensalzburg Fortress is a remarkable attraction that combines stunning views, rich history, and cultural experiences. Whether you're exploring its museums, enjoying the scenery, or simply soaking in the atmosphere, a visit to this fortress is sure to be a highlight of your time in Salzburg.

3.2 Mirabell Palace and Gardens

Overview

Mirabell Palace (*Schloss Mirabell*) is one of the most beautiful and historically significant landmarks in Salzburg. It is renowned for its stunning gardens, exquisite architecture, and rich history. The palace and its surrounding gardens attract visitors from all over the world, making it a must-see destination for anyone exploring Salzburg.

History of Mirabell Palace

The history of Mirabell Palace dates back to the early 18th century. It was originally built in 1606 by Prince-Archbishop Wolf Dietrich von Raitenau as a residence for his mistress, Salome Alt, and their children. The name "Mirabell" is derived from the Italian words "mira" (to admire) and "bella" (beautiful), reflecting the beauty of the palace and its gardens.

After the prince-archbishop's death in 1617, the palace underwent significant changes. His successor, Archbishop Markus Sittikus, expanded the palace and redesigned the gardens into the stunning formal landscape that we see today. The palace served as a summer residence for the archbishops and became a center for cultural events, gatherings, and celebrations.

Over the years, Mirabell Palace has seen many transformations and renovations, but it has retained its charm and historical significance. Today, it houses the Mirabell Palace Wedding Hall, where couples come to get married, and it is often used for concerts and cultural events, further cementing its role as a cultural hub in Salzburg.

Architecture of Mirabell Palace

The architecture of Mirabell Palace is a beautiful blend of Baroque and Rococo styles. The palace features elegant façades adorned with decorative elements, including statues, pilasters, and ornamental details. The main entrance is marked by a grand staircase, leading visitors into the heart of the palace.

Inside the palace, visitors can admire the opulent rooms that showcase the wealth and power of the archbishops. The Marble Hall (*Marmorsaal*) is one of the most stunning spaces in the palace. Its walls are adorned with beautiful marble, and the ceiling is painted with exquisite frescoes depicting mythological scenes. The hall is often used for concerts, and its exceptional acoustics make it a favorite venue for musical performances.

The Gardens of Mirabell

One of the most enchanting aspects of Mirabell Palace is its gardens, which are meticulously designed and beautifully maintained. The gardens are a prime example of formal Baroque garden design and are divided into several sections, each with its own distinct features.

1. **Main Garden:** The main garden is the most famous part of Mirabell. It features a symmetrical layout with neatly trimmed hedges, colorful flower beds, and beautiful pathways. At the center of the garden stands the iconic Pegasus Fountain, adorned with a statue of Pegasus, the winged horse from Greek mythology. The fountain is surrounded by vibrant flowerbeds, making it a popular spot for photos.
2. **Rose Garden:** Adjacent to the main garden is the serene Rose Garden, which boasts a stunning collection of over 200 varieties of roses. The fragrance of the roses fills the air, and the garden is a peaceful retreat where visitors can sit on benches and enjoy the beauty of nature. The Rose Garden is particularly lovely in late spring and summer when the flowers are in full bloom.
3. **Hedge Theatre:** One of the unique features of the gardens is the Hedge Theatre (*Hecken Theater*), an outdoor amphitheater created from meticulously trimmed hedges. The hedge theatre was designed for outdoor performances, providing a natural backdrop for concerts and theatrical events. Visitors can imagine the vibrant cultural life that once took place in this charming setting.
4. **Ornamental Gardens:** Beyond the main garden and rose garden, there are several ornamental gardens filled with a variety of plants, flowers, and sculptures. These gardens provide an excellent opportunity for leisurely walks and offer stunning views of the palace and the surrounding landscape.

Cultural Significance

Mirabell Palace and Gardens hold significant cultural importance in Salzburg. The palace is often featured in cultural events, concerts, and festivals. Its central location makes it a focal point for various activities, including music festivals, art exhibitions, and public celebrations.

The palace is also famous for its association with Wolfgang Amadeus Mozart. Mozart's father, Leopold, taught his children in the palace's gardens, and it is said that the composer himself enjoyed spending time in this beautiful setting. The connection to Mozart adds to the cultural richness of Mirabell and attracts music lovers from around the world.

Visiting Mirabell Palace and Gardens

Visiting Mirabell Palace and Gardens is a delightful experience that offers something for everyone. Here's what you need to know to make the most of your visit:

1. **Opening Hours:** Mirabell Palace is typically open to visitors year-round, but opening hours may vary depending on the season. The gardens are generally open to the public, allowing visitors to stroll through the lush landscapes at any time. It's advisable to check the official website for the most up-to-date information on opening hours.
2. **Admission Fees:** Entry to the gardens is free, making it accessible to all visitors. However, guided tours of the palace and certain events may require admission fees. Check ahead for any special exhibitions or performances that might be taking place during your visit.
3. **Guided Tours:** For a more in-depth understanding of the palace's history and architecture, consider joining a guided tour. Knowledgeable guides can share fascinating stories about the palace's past, the archbishops, and the gardens. Tours are available in multiple languages, ensuring that visitors from around the world can enjoy the experience.
4. **Accessibility:** Mirabell Palace and Gardens are generally accessible for visitors with mobility challenges. The gardens have well-maintained paths, and ramps are available to access the palace. However, some areas may have uneven surfaces, so it's advisable to be cautious.
5. **Photography:** The gardens and the palace offer countless opportunities for stunning photographs. Whether you're capturing the vibrant flowers, the elegant architecture, or the breathtaking views of the Alps in the background, Mirabell is a photographer's paradise. Just be respectful of other visitors while taking photos, especially in busier areas.
6. **Events and Concerts:** Check the schedule for concerts and events held in the palace and gardens. The Marble Hall often hosts classical music performances, while the gardens may feature outdoor concerts during the summer months. Attending an event adds a special touch to your visit, allowing you to experience the cultural vibrancy of Salzburg.

7. **Dining Options:** While there are no restaurants directly within the palace, you can find nearby cafés and eateries to enjoy a meal or a snack. Take a break in one of the nearby cafés and savor traditional Austrian pastries, coffee, or lunch before or after exploring the gardens.
8. **Seasonal Highlights:** Each season brings a different charm to Mirabell Palace and Gardens:
    - **Spring:** In spring, the gardens burst into color with blooming flowers and blossoming trees. The fragrance of flowers fills the air, making it a delightful time to visit.
    - **Summer:** Summer brings lush greenery and vibrant flower displays. The gardens are in full bloom, and outdoor concerts are often held in the evenings, adding to the lively atmosphere.
    - **Autumn:** In autumn, the gardens transform with rich fall colors, providing a picturesque setting for leisurely strolls. The cooler weather is perfect for exploring the grounds without the summer crowds.
    - **Winter:** Although the gardens are less colorful in winter, Mirabell Palace remains beautiful against a backdrop of snow. The palace itself is often decorated for the holiday season, making it a lovely spot for winter walks.

Tips for a Memorable Visit

- **Take Your Time:** Allow yourself plenty of time to explore both the palace and the gardens. Take leisurely walks, find a quiet bench to sit and relax, and soak in the beauty of your surroundings.
- **Pack a Picnic:** If the weather is nice, consider packing a picnic to enjoy in the gardens. There are plenty of beautiful spots to sit and eat, allowing you to make the most of your time in this picturesque setting.
- **Visit Nearby Attractions:** Mirabell Palace is conveniently located near other popular attractions, such as the Salzburg Cathedral and Getreidegasse. Consider planning your day to include these nearby sites, making it easy to explore more of what Salzburg has to offer.
- **Engage with Local Culture**: Look for any special events or exhibitions happening at the palace or in the gardens. Engaging with local culture adds depth to your visit and allows you to experience Salzburg's vibrant arts scene.

Conclusion

Mirabell Palace and Gardens are truly a gem in the heart of Salzburg. With their rich history, stunning architecture, and beautifully landscaped gardens, they offer a perfect blend of cultural significance and natural beauty. Whether you're wandering through the gardens, admiring the impressive palace, or attending a concert in the Marble Hall, you'll find plenty of reasons to fall in love with this enchanting location.

A visit to Mirabell is not just a sightseeing trip; it's an opportunity to immerse yourself in the beauty and history of Salzburg. So take your time, enjoy the views, and let the charm of Mirabell Palace and Gardens create lasting memories during your stay in this remarkable city.

3.3 Mozart's Birthplace

Overview

Mozart's Birthplace, known as *Mozarts Geburtshaus* in German, is one of the most significant cultural landmarks in Salzburg. Located in the heart of the old town of Getreidegasse, this historic building is where the world-renowned composer Wolfgang Amadeus Mozart was born on January 27, 1756. Today, the site serves as a museum dedicated to the life and works of Mozart, offering visitors an intimate glimpse into the early years of this musical genius.

History of Mozart's Birthplace

The building itself has a rich history. Constructed in 1497, it was a home and shop for various merchants before it became the residence of the Mozart family in 1747. At that time, Leopold Mozart, Wolfgang's father, was already a well-respected musician and composer. The family lived on the third floor of the house, where Wolfgang was born and spent his early childhood.

In 1773, the family moved to a larger residence on Makartplatz, but the building on Getreidegasse remained a significant site for admirers of Mozart. In 1880, the house was opened as a museum to celebrate Mozart's life and work. It has undergone various renovations and expansions over the years to enhance the visitor experience, while preserving its historical significance.

Exploring the Museum

The museum at Mozart's Birthplace is divided into several rooms and exhibits, each providing unique insights into the life of the composer and his family. Here's what you can expect to see:

1. **Family Rooms**: The museum features rooms that recreate the Mozart family's living space. Visitors can see how they lived during Wolfgang's early years, including original furniture, paintings, and artifacts that reflect their lifestyle. The rooms are designed to

give a sense of the environment in which Mozart grew up, fostering his musical talent from a young age.
2. **Exhibitions on Mozart's Life**: The museum contains a wealth of information about Mozart's early life, education, and family background. Exhibits detail his prodigious talent, which was evident from a young age. Visitors can explore documents, letters, and original manuscripts that showcase his early compositions and the influences that shaped his musical style.
3. **Instruments and Artifacts**: One of the highlights of the museum is the collection of musical instruments and artifacts belonging to Mozart and his family. This includes a keyboard that Mozart used, as well as various string instruments. The collection provides a fascinating look at the tools of his trade and the music he created.
4. **Personal Items**: The museum also displays personal items belonging to Mozart, such as his violin and letters. These artifacts help to humanize the composer, allowing visitors to connect with him on a personal level. You can see how he communicated with friends and family, providing a glimpse into his life beyond music.
5. **Interactive Exhibits**: The museum incorporates modern technology to enhance the visitor experience. Interactive displays allow guests to listen to Mozart's music, watch videos about his life, and engage with his compositions in a fun and informative way. These features make the museum appealing to visitors of all ages.
6. **Multimedia Presentations**: Throughout the museum, multimedia presentations provide context and background about Mozart's life and his impact on music history. Visitors can watch short films and presentations that delve into his significance as a composer and the legacy he left behind.

Visiting Mozart's Birthplace

A visit to Mozart's Birthplace is a highlight for music lovers and history enthusiasts alike. Here's what you need to know for an enjoyable experience:

1. **Opening Hours**: The museum is generally open year-round, but hours may vary depending on the season. It's best to check the official website for the latest information on opening times and any special events or closures.
2. **Admission Fees**: There is an admission fee to enter the museum. Ticket prices may vary for adults, students, and families. Combo tickets that include other Mozart-related sites, such as Mozart's Residence, are often available and can provide good value.
3. **Guided Tours**: To gain a deeper understanding of Mozart's life and his contributions to music, consider taking a guided tour. Knowledgeable guides share fascinating stories and insights, enhancing your appreciation of the exhibits. Tours are available in multiple languages.
4. **Audio Guides**: If you prefer to explore at your own pace, audio guides are often available for rent at the entrance. These guides provide detailed information about the

exhibits and the history of the building, allowing you to delve deeper into the life of Mozart.
5. **Accessibility**: The museum is accessible to visitors with mobility challenges, with ramps and elevators available to reach the various levels. However, some areas may have narrow passageways, so it's advisable to plan your visit accordingly.
6. **Photography**: Photography is generally allowed in most areas of the museum, but be respectful of other visitors and any specific restrictions that may be in place. Capturing the atmosphere and exhibits can help you remember your visit.
7. **Gift Shop**: Don't forget to visit the museum gift shop, where you can find a range of Mozart-themed souvenirs, including CDs of his music, books about his life, and various memorabilia. These items make great keepsakes or gifts for fellow music enthusiasts.
8. **Nearby Attractions**: Mozart's Birthplace is conveniently located near other notable attractions in Salzburg, including the **Salzburg Cathedral**, **Mirabell Palace**, and **Getreidegasse**. Consider planning your day to include visits to these nearby sites, making it easy to explore more of what the city has to offer.

Cultural Significance

Mozart's Birthplace holds immense cultural significance, not just for Salzburg, but for the entire world of classical music. As one of the most influential composers in Western music history, Mozart's works have shaped the musical landscape for centuries. His compositions, including symphonies, operas, and chamber music, continue to be performed and celebrated globally.

The museum serves as a pilgrimage site for music lovers and scholars, who come to pay homage to the composer and gain insights into his life. It also plays an essential role in promoting classical music and educating visitors about its history. The impact of Mozart's work is felt not only in concert halls but also in everyday culture, making the museum a vital part of Salzburg's identity.

Events and Celebrations

Mozart's Birthplace is often the site of special events and celebrations that honor the composer. Concerts, lectures, and workshops are held throughout the year, attracting musicians, scholars, and fans alike.

- **Mozart Week**: One of the most prominent events is *Mozart Week*, held annually in January to celebrate the composer's birthday. The festival features performances of his works by renowned orchestras, chamber groups, and soloists, bringing Mozart's music to life in the very city where he was born.
- **Educational Programs**: The museum also offers educational programs for students and music enthusiasts. These programs may include masterclasses, lectures, and guided tours

focusing on various aspects of Mozart's music and life. Engaging with these programs can deepen your appreciation for his genius and the impact of his work.

Conclusion

Mozart's Birthplace is not only a museum; it is a tribute to one of the greatest composers in history. Visiting this landmark provides an opportunity to connect with the life and legacy of Wolfgang Amadeus Mozart, immersing yourself in the environment that shaped his early years.

From exploring the beautifully preserved rooms to discovering the artifacts that tell the story of his life, every corner of the museum resonates with the spirit of Mozart. Whether you are a devoted fan of classical music or simply curious about this remarkable figure, a visit to Mozart's Birthplace will undoubtedly leave you with a deeper understanding of his influence and the enduring power of his music.

As you walk through the halls of this historic building, take a moment to reflect on the extraordinary talent that emerged from this humble abode. Mozart's legacy continues to inspire generations, and his birthplace remains a beacon of musical history in the beautiful city of Salzburg.

3.4 Salzburg Cathedral

Overview

Salzburg Cathedral, known as Salzburger *Dom* in German, is one of the most iconic landmarks in Salzburg and a masterpiece of Baroque architecture. Its magnificent dome and stunning façade dominate the city's skyline, making it a must-visit site for anyone exploring this charming city. The cathedral is not only a place of worship but also a significant cultural and historical symbol of Salzburg, reflecting the city's rich heritage and its strong ties to Christianity.

History of Salzburg Cathedral

The history of Salzburg Cathedral dates back to the early Christian era, but the current structure was built in the 17th century. The original cathedral, dedicated to St. Rupert, was established in the year 774, making it one of the oldest churches in the region. However, this structure suffered severe damage in a fire in 1598, prompting the need for a new cathedral.

The construction of the current Salzburg Cathedral began in 1614 under the direction of architect **Wolfgang Dietrich** and was completed in 1657. The cathedral was consecrated by Archbishop **Maximilian Gandolf von Kuenburg** in 1688. Its design showcases the grandeur of the Baroque style, characterized by elaborate decorations, dramatic forms, and a sense of movement and light.

Over the years, the cathedral has undergone several restorations and renovations, including a significant restoration after World War II when the building sustained damage from bombing raids. Today, Salzburg Cathedral stands as a testament to the resilience of the city and its commitment to preserving its architectural heritage.

Architecture of Salzburg Cathedral

The architecture of Salzburg Cathedral is a stunning example of Baroque design. Key features include:

1. **The Façade**: The cathedral's façade is characterized by its imposing structure, with two tall towers that rise majestically above the entrance. The exterior is adorned with intricate carvings and statues, including figures of saints that reflect the cathedral's religious significance.
2. **The Dome**: The most striking feature of the cathedral is its large dome, which rises to a height of 80 meters (about 262 feet). The dome is covered in a beautiful green copper patina, which gives it a distinct appearance. Inside, the dome is decorated with stunning frescoes depicting scenes from the life of Christ and the saints.
3. **Interior Design**: Upon entering the cathedral, visitors are greeted by a breathtaking interior filled with ornate decorations, colorful frescoes, and gilded altars. The nave is wide and airy, leading to the impressive altar area. The use of light, combined with the rich colors of the decorations, creates a serene and uplifting atmosphere.
4. **Altars and Chapels**: The cathedral features several altars and chapels, each dedicated to different saints. The high altar, designed by architect **Johann Bernhard Fischer von Erlach**, is a focal point of the interior and is adorned with a magnificent altarpiece depicting the baptism of Christ.
5. **Organ**: The cathedral is home to a magnificent organ, which is one of the largest in Austria. It has more than 4,000 pipes and is a centerpiece of many musical performances held in the cathedral. The organ is often used for services and concerts, showcasing its exceptional sound.

Cultural Significance

Salzburg Cathedral is not only a place of worship but also a cultural center for the city. It plays a vital role in the religious life of Salzburg and hosts various liturgical events throughout the year, including Christmas masses, Easter celebrations, and other significant religious occasions.

The cathedral is also closely associated with the life of Wolfgang Amadeus Mozart, who was baptized here. Mozart's family attended services in the cathedral, and he composed several sacred works that were performed in this hallowed space. The connection to Mozart adds to the cathedral's cultural richness, making it an essential part of Salzburg's musical heritage.

Visiting Salzburg Cathedral

A visit to Salzburg Cathedral is a memorable experience that offers a glimpse into the city's religious and architectural history. Here are some essential tips for making the most of your visit:

1. **Opening Hours**: Salzburg Cathedral is generally open to visitors year-round, but hours may vary based on religious services and special events. It's advisable to check the official website for up-to-date information on visiting hours.
2. **Admission Fees**: Entry to the cathedral is typically free, although donations are appreciated to help with maintenance and preservation efforts. However, certain areas, such as the dome and crypt, may have a small admission fee.
3. **Guided Tours**: To gain a deeper understanding of the cathedral's history, architecture, and significance, consider joining a guided tour. Knowledgeable guides can provide valuable insights and share fascinating stories about the cathedral's past. Tours are often available in multiple languages.
4. **Audio Guides**: For visitors who prefer to explore at their own pace, audio guides may be available for rent. These guides offer detailed explanations of the cathedral's features, history, and artistic elements.
5. **Dress Code**: As Salzburg Cathedral is a place of worship, visitors are encouraged to dress modestly. This means avoiding overly revealing clothing and ensuring that shoulders and knees are covered. Respecting the dress code enhances the experience and shows reverence for the sacred space.
6. **Photography**: Photography is generally allowed inside the cathedral, but visitors should be respectful of others and avoid using flash, especially during services. Capturing the beauty of the architecture and artwork is encouraged, but be mindful of the serene atmosphere.
7. **Accessibility**: Salzburg Cathedral is accessible to visitors with mobility challenges. Ramps and elevators are available, making it easier for everyone to explore the interior. However, be aware that some areas may have uneven surfaces.
8. **Events and Concerts**: The cathedral frequently hosts concerts and special events, especially during the summer months and around holidays. Attending a concert can be a unique way to experience the cathedral's acoustics and enjoy the beauty of Mozart's music in the very space where it was performed centuries ago.
9. **Nearby Attractions**: The cathedral is centrally located in Salzburg, making it easy to combine your visit with other nearby attractions. Consider exploring the **Residenza Palace**, the **Mozart's Birthplace**, or taking a stroll through the picturesque streets of the old town.

Events and Festivals

Throughout the year, Salzburg Cathedral hosts various events and festivals that highlight its cultural and religious significance:

- **Easter Services**: The cathedral is particularly vibrant during the Easter season, with special services that attract locals and visitors alike. The atmosphere is filled with music, prayer, and celebration, making it a beautiful time to experience the cathedral's spiritual essence.
- **Christmas Mass**: One of the most popular events is the Christmas Mass, where thousands gather to celebrate the holiday season. The cathedral is beautifully decorated, and the sound of choirs fills the air, creating a magical experience.
- **Summer Concerts**: During the summer months, the cathedral hosts a series of classical concerts featuring local and international musicians. The acoustics of the space provide an extraordinary backdrop for performances of both sacred and secular music.

Conclusion

Salzburg Cathedral stands as a magnificent testament to the city's rich history, culture, and religious heritage. Its stunning Baroque architecture, vibrant interior, and deep connections to notable figures like Wolfgang Amadeus Mozart make it an essential stop for anyone visiting Salzburg.

Whether you are drawn by the beauty of its design, the historical significance of the site, or the opportunity to experience live music in a breathtaking setting, a visit to Salzburg Cathedral is sure to leave a lasting impression. Take your time to explore its many features, soak in the serene atmosphere, and reflect on the centuries of history that have unfolded within its walls.

As you stand beneath the grand dome, surrounded by the intricate artwork and the echo of Mozart's melodies, you will understand why Salzburg Cathedral is not only a place of worship but also a symbol of the city's enduring spirit and its rich musical heritage.

3.5 Sound of Music Tour Highlights

Overview

The Sound of Music is not just a film; it's a beloved cultural phenomenon that has captured the hearts of millions around the world. Set against the breathtaking backdrop of Salzburg, the film showcases the stunning landscapes, charming architecture, and rich musical heritage of the region. For fans of the movie, a *Sound of Music* tour in Salzburg offers a unique opportunity to explore the locations featured in the film while learning about its history and the real-life von Trapp family. This chapter highlights the key attractions and experiences that make this tour a must-do for visitors.

The von Trapp Family and the Film

Before diving into the tour highlights, it's essential to understand the connection between the *Sound of Music* and the von Trapp family. The film, released in 1965 and based on the memoir *The Story of the Trapp Family Singers*, tells the story of Maria, a spirited young woman who becomes a governess for the widowed Captain Georg von Trapp and his seven children. The family's journey through love, music, and courage during the rise of the Nazi regime in Austria is both inspiring and heartwarming.

Tour Overview

The *Sound of Music* tour typically lasts around 4 to 5 hours, and various companies offer guided excursions, allowing visitors to relax and soak in the beautiful scenery without worrying about logistics. Most tours include transportation to key filming locations, along with informative commentary from knowledgeable guides who share fascinating stories about the film and the real von Trapp family.

Here are some of the highlights you can expect during the tour:

1. Mirabell Palace and Gardens

The tour often begins at the stunning Mirabell Palace, where several iconic scenes from the film were shot. The gardens, with their beautifully manicured hedges and vibrant flowers, served as the backdrop for the memorable "Do-Re-Mi" song sequence.

- **Key Features**: As you stroll through the gardens, look for the *Pegasus Fountain* and the *Dwarf Garden*, both featured in the film. The gardens offer a picturesque setting for photos, and the surrounding views of the fortress make for a perfect backdrop.
- **Experience**: Many tours allow time for guests to explore the gardens on foot, so take the opportunity to relive your favorite moments from the film while enjoying the beauty of the flowers and the serene atmosphere.

2. St. Peter's Cemetery

Next, the tour often includes a visit to *St. Peter's Cemetery*, one of the oldest cemeteries in Salzburg. The cemetery played a pivotal role in the film, particularly during the scene where the von Trapp family seeks refuge from the Nazis.

- **Key Features**: As you walk through the cemetery, admire the ornate tombstones and the stunning baroque architecture of the surrounding buildings. The peaceful atmosphere of this site contrasts sharply with the tension of the scenes filmed here.
- **Experience**: Listen to your guide share stories about the history of the cemetery and its significance in the film, enhancing your appreciation for the location's beauty and the poignant moments captured on film.

3. Nonnberg Abbey

Nonnberg Abbey is another significant location on the tour, as it is where Maria was a postulant before becoming the von Trapp children's governess. The abbey's beautiful architecture and serene gardens make it a highlight of the tour.

- **Key Features**: The abbey, founded in the 8th century, is still home to a community of nuns. While you can't enter the abbey itself, the exterior is stunning and offers a glimpse into the life of the nuns and the inspiration for Maria's character.

- **Experience**: Guides often share anecdotes about how the abbey's setting influenced the film and how it represents Maria's journey of faith and self-discovery.

4. Leopoldskron Palace

Leopoldskron Palace is another stunning site featured in the film, serving as the exterior of the von Trapp family's home. The palace's picturesque setting on the shores of a lake, with the backdrop of the mountains, creates a breathtaking view.

- **Key Features**: The palace, built in the 18th century, boasts beautiful gardens and a serene lake. The impressive Rococo architecture adds to the romantic charm of the location.
- **Experience**: While the palace is privately owned and not open to the public, the view from the lakeside is worth stopping for. Many tours provide opportunities for photos, allowing you to capture the essence of the von Trapp family home.

5. Hellbrunn Palace

Hellbrunn Palace is often included in the tour itinerary due to its beautiful gardens and unique trick fountains. While it wasn't a filming location, it is worth visiting for its stunning landscape and the fun experience it offers.

- **Key Features**: The gardens are beautifully landscaped, and the trick fountains provide a whimsical touch. Visitors can enjoy a guided tour of the palace, which includes entertaining anecdotes about its history.
- **Experience**: Take a break from the film-focused sites and enjoy a lighthearted experience in the gardens, making it a perfect spot for families or anyone looking to add some fun to their day.

6. Sound of Music Film Locations

Throughout the tour, your guide will point out various film locations around Salzburg, including picturesque streets and buildings that served as backdrops for many scenes.

- **Key Features**: Look out for the iconic *Maria's Bike Ride* scene location, where she joyfully sings while cycling through the beautiful Austrian countryside.
- **Experience**: Some tours may include singing along to favorite *Sound of Music* songs during the drive, enhancing the fun atmosphere and allowing fans to relive the film's joyous moments.

7. Scenic Drives and Views

One of the most delightful aspects of the tour is the scenic drive through the Austrian countryside. The rolling hills, majestic mountains, and lush landscapes create a stunning backdrop that mirrors the film's enchanting visuals.

- **Key Features**: As you travel between locations, take in the breathtaking views of the Alps and picturesque villages that add to the charm of Salzburg.
- **Experience**: Many tours offer photo stops at scenic viewpoints, allowing you to capture the beauty of the region and the spirit of the film.

Conclusion

The *Sound of Music* tour is a magical experience that brings the beloved film to life while showcasing the breathtaking beauty of Salzburg. Whether you are a die-hard fan of the movie or simply looking to explore the stunning landscapes of this charming city, the tour offers a unique blend of history, culture, and entertainment.

By visiting iconic locations like Mirabell Palace, St. Peter's Cemetery, and Leopoldskron Palace, you will gain a deeper appreciation for the film and the real-life von Trapp family. The combination of stunning scenery, engaging stories, and the chance to relive memorable film moments makes this tour an unforgettable highlight of your time in Salzburg.

As you sing along to the songs of the film and soak in the beautiful landscapes, you will understand why *The Sound of Music* continues to resonate with audiences around the world, celebrating themes of love, family, and the power of music.

Local Cuisine

4.1 Traditional Dishes to Try

Salzburg, nestled in the heart of Austria, is known not only for its stunning architecture and rich history but also for its delicious local cuisine. When visiting this charming city, indulging in traditional dishes is a must to experience the true flavors of Austrian culture. This chapter will guide you through some of the most popular traditional dishes to try during your stay in Salzburg.

1. Wiener Schnitzel

Wiener Schnitzel is perhaps the most famous dish associated with Austrian cuisine. This iconic meal consists of a breaded and fried veal cutlet, served with a lemon wedge, potato salad, or parsley potatoes.

- **Taste & Texture**: The schnitzel is crispy on the outside and tender on the inside, offering a delightful contrast in texture. The lemon adds a refreshing touch that balances the richness of the fried coating.
- **Where to Try**: Many traditional restaurants in Salzburg serve Wiener Schnitzel, including *St. Peter Stiftskeller*, one of the oldest restaurants in the city. Be sure to sample this dish to get a true taste of Austria.

2. Salzburger Nockerl

Salzburger Nockerl is a sweet dish that pays homage to Salzburg's beauty. This dessert consists of a fluffy soufflé made from egg whites, sugar, and flour, baked to perfection and served warm.

- **Taste & Texture**: Light and airy, the Nockerl has a delicate sweetness and a slightly crispy exterior, giving way to a soft and pillowy inside. It is often dusted with powdered sugar and served with a berry sauce or vanilla cream.
- **Where to Try**: For a truly authentic experience, head to *Café Tomaselli*, one of Salzburg's oldest coffee houses, where you can enjoy this delightful dessert while soaking in the historic ambiance.

3. Tafelspitz

Tafelspitz is a classic Austrian dish that consists of boiled beef, traditionally served with broth, root vegetables, and horseradish sauce. This hearty meal is a favorite among locals and reflects the country's love for comfort food.

- **Taste & Texture**: The meat is tender and flavorful, while the broth is rich and nourishing. The addition of horseradish adds a spicy kick that enhances the overall experience.
- **Where to Try**: Try Tafelspitz at *Restaurant S'Kloane Brauhaus*, known for its traditional Austrian dishes and cozy atmosphere.

4. Kasnocken (Cheese Noodles)

Kasnocken is a delightful dish made from small dumplings similar to spaetzle, which are tossed with melted cheese and often topped with crispy onions.

- **Taste & Texture**: The noodles are soft and chewy, while the cheese adds a creamy richness. The crispy onions provide a delightful crunch, making each bite a satisfying experience.
- **Where to Try**: Visit *Die Weisse*, a popular brewery restaurant in Salzburg, to savor authentic Kasnocken paired with a local .

5. Apfelstrudel

Apfelstrudel, or apple strudel, is a classic Austrian pastry that has gained popularity worldwide. Made from thin layers of dough filled with spiced apples, raisins, and cinnamon, it's typically served warm with a dusting of powdered sugar and a side of vanilla sauce or whipped cream.

- **Taste & Texture**: The strudel has a crispy outer layer, while the filling is sweet and aromatic, with a perfect balance of flavors. The combination of textures creates a delightful dessert experience.
- **Where to Try**: Enjoy a slice of Apfelstrudel at *Café Mozart*, where they serve it fresh from the oven. Pair it with a cup of coffee for the ultimate treat.

6. Speckplatte (Cured Meat Platter)

A Speckplatte is a traditional Austrian platter featuring a selection of cured meats, including bacon, sausages, and ham, often served with pickles, bread, and cheese.

- **Taste & Texture**: Each type of meat offers a unique flavor, with the smoky and salty characteristics of the cured meats balanced by the tanginess of pickles. The platter is a perfect appetizer or snack to share.
- **Where to Try**: Sample a Speckplatte at *Augustiner Bräu*, a historic brewery in Salzburg where you can enjoy this dish in a lively garden atmosphere.

7. Brettljause (Austrian Snack Board)

Brettljause is a hearty Austrian snack board that typically includes a variety of cured meats, cheeses, pickled vegetables, and fresh bread. **Taste & Texture**: The combination of flavors from the meats and cheeses, along with the crunch of pickled vegetables, creates a satisfying and savory experience.

- **Where to Try**: Many taverns and gardens in Salzburg offer Brettljause. Check out *Wirtshaus zum Hirschen* for a cozy atmosphere and delicious selections.

8. Frittatensuppe (Pancake Soup)

Frittatensuppe is a comforting soup made from a clear broth, served with thin strips of savory pancakes (frittaten) added to the bowl.

- **Taste & Texture**: The broth is light and flavorful, while the pancake strips add a unique twist and texture to the dish. It's a popular starter in many traditional Austrian meals.
- **Where to Try**: Enjoy Frittatensuppe at *Blaue Gans*, a restaurant that blends traditional cuisine with a modern touch.

Conclusion

Salzburg offers a rich culinary landscape that reflects its Austrian heritage and local traditions. From hearty dishes like Wiener Schnitzel and Tafelspitz to delightful desserts like Salzburger Nockerl and Apfelstrudel, there is something for every palate to enjoy. Be sure to indulge in these traditional dishes during your visit to experience the authentic flavors of Salzburg and immerse yourself in the local culture.

As you explore the city's charming streets and historical sites, let the local cuisine enhance your travel experience, allowing you to savor the delicious tastes that define this beautiful region. Whether dining in a cozy café or a bustling restaurant, each dish tells a story of tradition and love for food, making your visit to Salzburg truly unforgettable.

4.2 Best Restaurants and Cafés

Salzburg is a culinary delight, with a variety of restaurants and cafés that serve both traditional Austrian dishes and international cuisine. Whether you're looking for a cozy café to enjoy a cup of coffee and a slice of cake or a fine dining experience, Salzburg has something for everyone. Here's a comprehensive guide to some of the best restaurants and cafés in the city, including their prices, addresses, and contact information.

1. St. Peter Stiftskeller

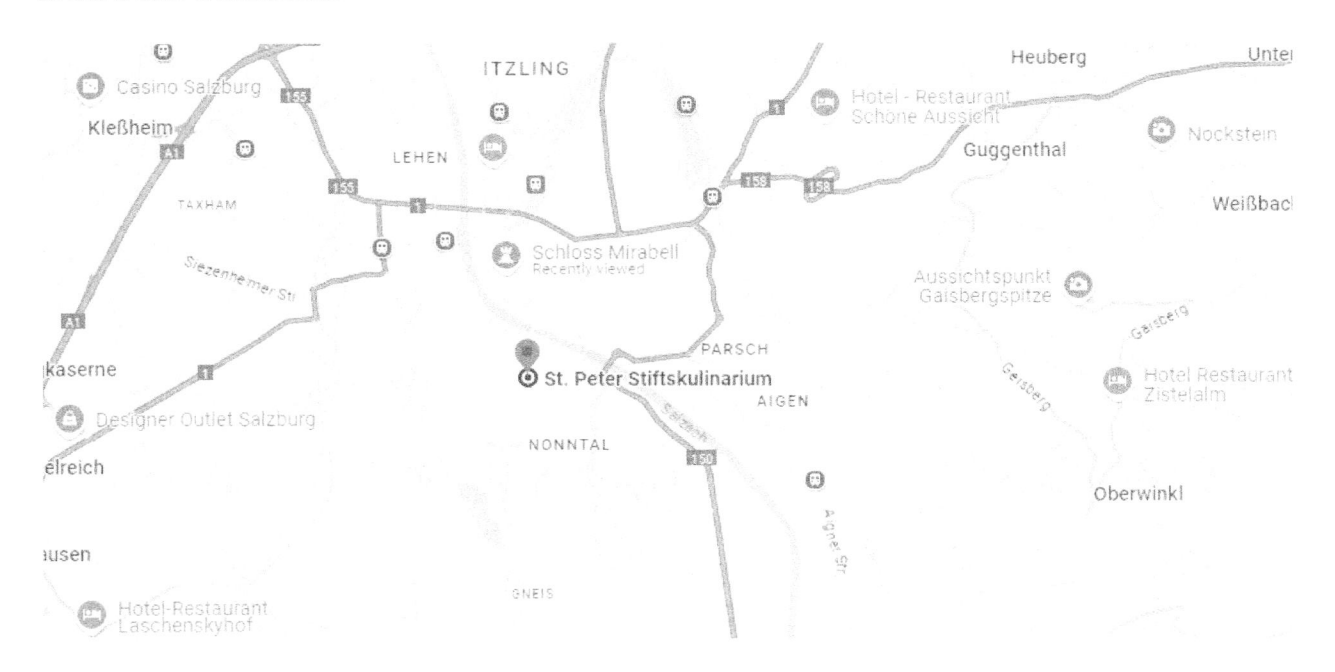

Overview: Located in a historic building dating back to the year 803, St. Peter Stiftskeller is one of the oldest restaurants in Europe. The ambiance is charming, with beautiful medieval architecture and a cozy atmosphere. It offers a delightful mix of traditional Austrian and international cuisine.

- **Must-Try Dishes**: Wiener Schnitzel, Salzburger Nockerl, and Tafelspitz.
- **Price Range**: €20 - €45 per person.
- **Address**: St. Peter Bezirk 1, 5020 Salzburg, Austria.
- **Contact**: +43 662 84 82 28
- **Website**: www.stpeter-stiftskeller.at

2. Café Tomaselli

Overview: Café Tomaselli is one of the oldest coffee houses in Salzburg, founded in 1700. It's a perfect spot to relax and enjoy a coffee, pastry, or light meal. The café has a lovely outdoor seating area where you can watch the world go by.

- **Must-Try Dishes**: Apfelstrudel, Sacher Torte, and a variety of Austrian coffee specialties.
- **Price Range**: €5 - €15 per person.
- **Address**: Alter Markt 9, 5020 Salzburg, Austria.

- **Contact**: +43 662 84 45 45
- **Website**: www.tomaselli.at

3. Restaurant S'Kloane Brauhaus

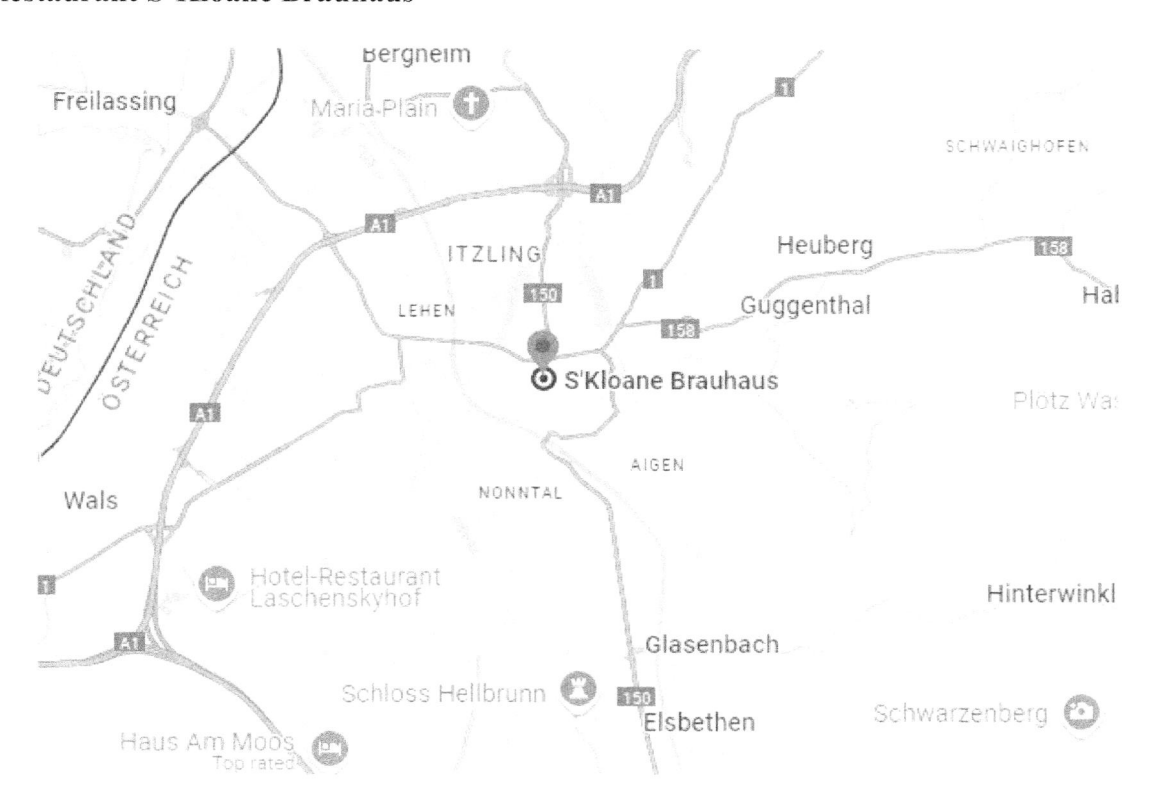

Overview: This brewery restaurant offers a rustic atmosphere and is known for its authentic Austrian dishes. The house-brewed pairs perfectly with the hearty meals served here.

- **Must-Try Dishes**: Tafelspitz, Goulash, and various sausages.
- **Price Range**: €15 - €30 per person.
- **Address**: Linzer Gasse 41, 5020 Salzburg, Austria.
- **Contact**: +43 662 87 20 06
- **Website**: www.brauhaus-salzburg.at

4. Die Weisse

Overview: Known for its casual and friendly atmosphere, Die Weisse is a popular brewery restaurant. It serves a wide variety of traditional Austrian dishes and is famous for its .

- **Must-Try Dishes**: Kasnocken, Wiener Schnitzel, and Speckplatte.
- **Price Range**: €10 - €25 per person.
- **Address**: Rupertgasse 10, 5020 Salzburg, Austria.
- **Contact**: +43 662 87 19 77
- **Website**: www.dieweisse.at

5. Blaue Gans

Overview: Located in the historic old town, Blaue Gans offers a mix of traditional and modern Austrian cuisine. The restaurant has a stylish interior and a lovely outdoor terrace.

- **Must-Try Dishes**: Frittatensuppe, seasonal salads, and fresh fish dishes.
- **Price Range**: €15 - €40 per person.
- **Address**: Blasius-Huber-Gasse 5, 5020 Salzburg, Austria.
- **Contact**: +43 662 84 11 55
- **Website**: www.blauegans.at

6. Augustiner Bräu

Overview: Augustiner Bräu is a well-known brewery that offers a lively atmosphere, perfect for enjoying a casual meal and local . The garden is a favorite among locals and visitors alike.

- **Must-Try Dishes**: Brettljause, Wiener Schnitzel, and various seasonal dishes.
- **Price Range**: €10 - €25 per person.
- **Address**: Augustiner Bräu, Bräuhausstraße 9, 5020 Salzburg, Austria.
- **Contact**: +43 662 43 36 50
- **Website**: www.augustiner-braeu.at

7. Gasthof Goldene Ente

Overview: This charming restaurant is located in the heart of Salzburg and offers a cozy, traditional atmosphere. It serves a variety of Austrian dishes with a focus on quality ingredients.

- **Must-Try Dishes**: Pork knuckle, Salzburger Nockerl, and homemade desserts.
- **Price Range**: €15 - €35 per person.
- **Address**: Goldene Ente, Judengasse 15, 5020 Salzburg, Austria.
- **Contact**: +43 662 84 35 62
- **Website**: www.goldene-ente.at

8. Café Wernbacher

Overview: Café Wernbacher is a lovely café and restaurant located on the banks of the Salzach River. It's a great place to enjoy a meal or a coffee while taking in the beautiful views.

- **Must-Try Dishes**: Cakes, pastries, and light meals.
- **Price Range**: €5 - €20 per person.
- **Address**: Schwarzstraße 32, 5020 Salzburg, Austria.
- **Contact**: +43 662 84 27 37
- **Website**: www.wernbacher.com

9. Restaurant Schloss Aigen

Overview: Located in a beautiful castle, this restaurant offers a unique dining experience with elegant interiors and a stunning terrace. It specializes in fine dining and seasonal dishes.

- **Must-Try Dishes**: Creative seasonal menus and gourmet dishes.
- **Price Range**: €30 - €60 per person.
- **Address**: Aigener Straße 1, 5026 Salzburg, Austria.
- **Contact**: +43 662 43 40 41
- **Website**: www.schloss-aigen.at

10. Café Central

Overview: This historic café is known for its elegant ambiance and delicious pastries. It's a perfect spot for a coffee break after exploring the city.

- **Must-Try Dishes**: Sachertorte, Apfelstrudel, and various coffee specialties.
- **Price Range**: €5 - €15 per person.
- **Address**: Zibeltalstraße 1, 5020 Salzburg, Austria.
- **Contact**: +43 662 84 23 66
- **Website**: www.cafecentral.at

Conclusion

Salzburg offers a diverse range of dining options, from traditional Austrian cuisine to modern international dishes. Whether you're looking for a fine dining experience or a cozy café, there's something for everyone to enjoy. Be sure to explore these recommended restaurants and cafés to savor the flavors of Salzburg and make your visit truly memorable.

4.3 Food Markets and Street Food

Exploring Salzburg's food markets and street food is a delightful way to experience the local culture and flavors. These markets and vendors offer a variety of fresh produce, traditional delicacies, and quick bites that capture the essence of Austrian cuisine. Here's a comprehensive guide to the best food markets and street food options in Salzburg, including what to try and where to find them.

1. Salzburg Farmers' Market (Salzburger Wochenmarkt)

Overview: The Salzburg Farmers' Market takes place every Thursday and Saturday in the heart of the city at the Mirabellplatz. This bustling market is a great place to find fresh, local produce, meats, cheeses, and baked goods.

- **What to Try**: Look for seasonal fruits and vegetables, artisanal cheeses, freshly baked bread, and local meats. Don't miss the opportunity to sample some homemade jams and honey.
- **Opening Hours**: Thursdays and Saturdays from 7:00 AM to 1:30 PM.
- **Location**: Mirabellplatz, 5020 Salzburg, Austria.
- **Tip**: Arrive early to get the best selection and enjoy the lively atmosphere as local vendors set up their stalls.

2. Grünmarkt (Green Market)

Overview: The Grünmarkt is a charming market located in the Stadtteil (district) of Andräviertel. It's known for its vibrant atmosphere and a wide variety of fresh produce, herbs, and flowers.

- **What to Try**: Sample fresh herbs, organic vegetables, and local specialties such as cheese and cured meats. Many vendors offer ready-to-eat options, including salads and sandwiches.
- **Opening Hours**: Monday to Saturday from 7:00 AM to 1:00 PM.
- **Location**: Franz-Josef-Straße 24, 5020 Salzburg, Austria.
- **Tip**: Take your time to explore the stalls and chat with local vendors. Many are passionate about their products and happy to share tips on how to use them in your cooking.

3. Franziskaner Markt

Overview: Located near the historic Franziskaner monastery, this market is a hidden gem known for its fresh, local produce and artisanal products. It has a relaxed atmosphere and is frequented by locals.

- **What to Try**: In addition to fruits and vegetables, look for handmade crafts, organic products, and baked goods.
- **Opening Hours**: Monday to Saturday from 7:00 AM to 1:00 PM.
- **Location**: Franziskanergasse 1, 5020 Salzburg, Austria.
- **Tip**: Visit during lunchtime when local vendors often sell quick, delicious meals. You can grab a bite and enjoy it in the nearby square.

4. Street Food at the Old Town

Overview: Salzburg's Old Town (Altstadt) is not just famous for its beautiful architecture; it also offers a variety of street food options. As you stroll through the narrow streets, you'll find numerous food stalls and vendors selling tasty treats.

- **What to Try**: Sample the famous **Bosna**, a spicy sausage in a bun topped with onions and mustard, or indulge in **Käsekrainer**, a cheese-filled sausage that is grilled to perfection. For something sweet, try **Churros** or **Palatschinken** (Austrian pancakes) filled with jam or Nutella.
- **Location**: Look for vendors around the Getreidegasse, the main shopping street in the Old Town.
- **Tip**: Street food is a great way to grab a quick meal while exploring. Pair your food with a refreshing local from one of the nearby pubs or cafés.

5. The Food Truck Scene

Overview: In recent years, Salzburg has seen a rise in food trucks offering a variety of cuisines. These mobile kitchens provide a fun and casual dining experience, perfect for trying something new.

- **What to Try**: Food trucks often serve gourmet burgers, international street food, vegetarian options, and creative desserts. Look for trucks that serve **Falafel**, **Tacos**, or **Asian Fusion** dishes.
- **Location**: Food trucks can usually be found at events, festivals, and popular tourist spots throughout the city, especially during the warmer months.
- **Tip**: Follow local social media pages or websites to find out where food trucks will be stationed. They often post their locations and menus, making it easier to plan your food adventures.

6. Winter and Christmas Markets

Overview: If you visit Salzburg during the winter holiday season, the Christmas markets are a must-visit. These markets, usually held in the city center, feature festive decorations, crafts, and delicious food options.

- **What to Try**: Indulge in traditional holiday treats like **Lebkuchen** (gingerbread), roasted chestnuts, and **Glühwein** Warm potato pancakes and festive pastries are also popular.
- **Opening Hours**: Typically open from late November until Christmas Eve.
- **Location**: The main Christmas market is located at the Domplatz (Cathedral Square).
- **Tip**: Enjoy the festive atmosphere with live music and local crafts while you sip on your Glühwein and snack on delicious treats.

Conclusion

Exploring the food markets and street food scene in Salzburg is a fantastic way to immerse yourself in the local culture and culinary traditions. Whether you're sampling fresh produce at the farmers' market or indulging in savory street food in the Old Town, the city offers a delightful variety of flavors to enjoy. Be sure to take your time, try different dishes, and embrace the vibrant food culture that Salzburg has to offer.

Accommodation

5.1 Recommended Hotels and Hostels

Finding the right place to stay in Salzburg is essential for a comfortable and enjoyable trip. The city offers a wide range of accommodation options, from luxury hotels to budget-friendly hostels. Here's a comprehensive guide to some of the best recommended hotels and hostels in Salzburg, complete with prices, addresses, and contact information.

1. Hotel Elefant

Overview: Hotel Elefant is a charming boutique hotel located in the heart of Salzburg's Old Town. It's just a short walk from many major attractions, including Mozart's Birthplace and the Salzburg Cathedral. The hotel offers modern comforts while retaining its historic charm.

- Price Range: €120 - €200 per night.
- Address: Sigmund-Haffner-Gasse 4, 5020 Salzburg, Austria.
- Contact: +43 662 84 28 34
- Website: www.hotelelefant.at

2. Hotel Bristol Salzburg

Overview: This luxurious hotel is known for its elegant decor and excellent service. Located near Mirabell Palace and Gardens, Hotel Bristol offers stunning views of the city and the Alps. The hotel has a fine dining restaurant and a cozy bar.

- Price Range: €200 - €400 per night.
- Address: Makartplatz 2, 5020 Salzburg, Austria.
- Contact: +43 662 87 20 00
- Website: www.bristol-salzburg.at

3. Hotel Mozart

Overview: Situated in a quiet area, Hotel Mozart offers a comfortable and welcoming atmosphere. It's just a short walk from the city center and offers a mix of modern and traditional Austrian style. The hotel features a lovely garden and a cozy breakfast room.

- Price Range: €100 - €180 per night.
- Address: Marko-Feingold-Straße 2, 5020 Salzburg, Austria.
- Contact: +43 662 84 12 54
- Website: www.hotelmozart.at

4. Hotel Amadeus

Overview: Hotel Amadeus is a family-run hotel located in the heart of Salzburg. The hotel offers comfortable rooms, a delicious breakfast buffet, and a friendly atmosphere. It's within walking distance of many attractions and public transportation.

- Price Range: €90 - €160 per night.
- Address: Gabelsbergerstraße 2, 5020 Salzburg, Austria.
- Contact: +43 662 88 43 22
- Website: www.hotel-amadeus.at

5. MEININGER Hotel Salzburg City Center

Overview: This modern hostel is perfect for budget travelers. MEININGER Hotel offers both private rooms and dormitories. It's located along the banks of the Salzach River and is a short walk from the city center.

- Price Range: €20 - €100 per night.
- Address: Fürbergstraße 18-20, 5020 Salzburg, Austria.
- Contact: +43 720 88 52 72
- Website: www.meininger-hotels.com

6. Hostel Salzburg

Overview: Located in a vibrant neighborhood, Hostel Salzburg is known for its friendly atmosphere and social vibe. The hostel features a communal kitchen, lounge areas, and organized activities for guests. It's an excellent choice for young travelers and backpackers.

- Price Range: €15 - €40 per night.
- Address: Rudolfskai 42, 5020 Salzburg, Austria.
- Contact: +43 662 87 15 88
- Website: www.hostelsalzburg.com

7. Hotel Villa Carlton

Overview: Hotel Villa Carlton is a stylish boutique hotel located close to the city center. It offers a blend of modern amenities and traditional Austrian hospitality. The hotel has a lovely garden and a wellness area for guests to enjoy.

- Price Range: €150 - €250 per night.
- Address: Elisabethstraße 1, 5020 Salzburg, Austria.
- Contact: +43 662 87 80 00
- Website: www.villacarlton.at

8. The Pitter Hotel Salzburg

Overview: The Pitter Hotel is a well-known establishment with a long history in Salzburg. It features modern rooms, a rooftop terrace with stunning views, and a popular restaurant serving local cuisine. The hotel is located near the Mirabell Palace.

- Price Range: €130 - €250 per night.
- Address: Rainerstraße 6, 5020 Salzburg, Austria.
- Contact: +43 662 88 10 10
- Website: www.pitterhotel.com

9. Austria Trend Hotel Ananas Salzburg

Overview: This large hotel offers comfortable accommodations and a range of amenities, including a restaurant, fitness center, and sauna. It's conveniently located near the city center and public transportation.

- Price Range: €80 - €150 per night.
- Address: Alfred-Gruber-Straße 5, 5020 Salzburg, Austria.
- Contact: +43 662 43 01 10
- Website: www.austria-trend.at

10. Hotel Garni Hohensalzburg

Overview: A charming family-run hotel, Hotel Garni Hohensalzburg offers cozy accommodations with stunning views of the fortress. The hotel is located in a quiet area, making it perfect for relaxation while being close to the city's attractions.

- Price Range: €70 - €130 per night.
- Address: Mönchsberg 2, 5020 Salzburg, Austria.
- Contact: +43 662 84 16 86
- Website: www.hohensalzburg.com

Conclusion

Salzburg offers a wide range of accommodation options to suit different budgets and preferences. Whether you're looking for luxury, comfort, or a budget-friendly hostel, you'll find something that meets your needs. Consider the locations, amenities, and price ranges when choosing your accommodation, and you're sure to have a wonderful stay in this beautiful city.

5.2 Unique Stays (e.g., Boutique Hotels)

For travelers looking for something special during their visit to Salzburg, boutique hotels and unique accommodations offer a chance to experience the city in a distinctive way. These places often feature unique designs, personalized service, and a local touch that sets them apart from standard hotels. Here's a guide to some of the best unique stays in Salzburg, including price ranges, addresses, and contact information.

1. Hotel Goldener Hirsch

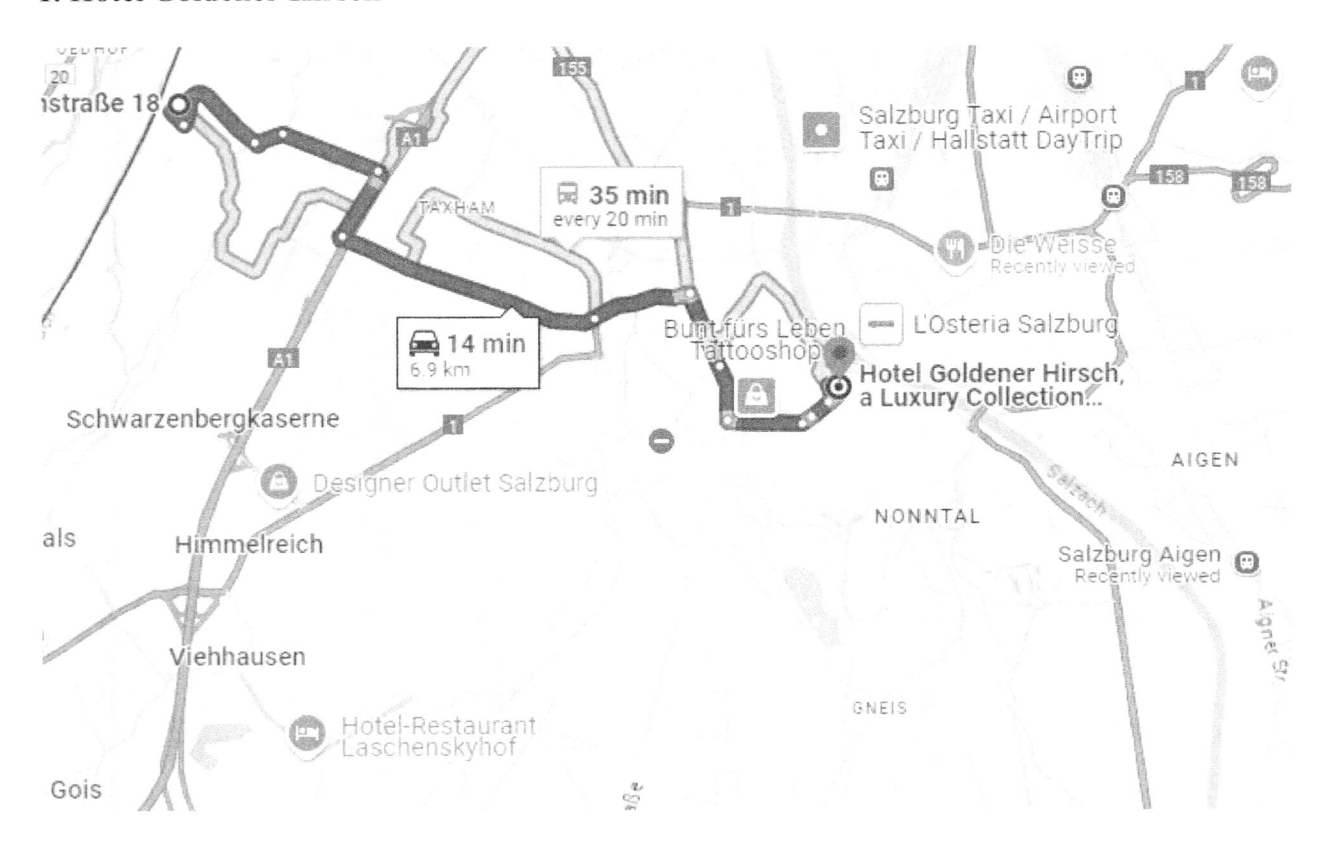

Overview: Hotel Goldener Hirsch is a beautifully restored hotel that exudes charm and elegance. Situated in the heart of Salzburg's Old Town, this historic hotel has welcomed guests since 1407. The interior features traditional Austrian decor and luxurious furnishings, providing a warm and inviting atmosphere.

- **Price Range**: €200 - €400 per night.
- **Address**: Getreidegasse 37, 5020 Salzburg, Austria.
- **Contact**: +43 662 80 00 80
- **Website**: www.goldenerhirsch.com

2. Hotel Elefant

Overview: A blend of tradition and modernity, Hotel Elefant is known for its unique design and personalized service. Located in the Old Town, it offers easy access to local attractions. The hotel features cozy rooms, a lovely courtyard, and a rich history that adds to its charm.

- **Price Range**: €120 - €200 per night.
- **Address**: Sigmund-Haffner-Gasse 4, 5020 Salzburg, Austria.
- **Contact**: +43 662 84 28 34
- **Website**: www.hotelelefant.at

3. Hotel Brunnauer

Overview: Hotel Brunnauer is a family-run boutique hotel that combines a modern aesthetic with a warm, welcoming atmosphere. It features stylish rooms and a beautiful garden area. Located near the city center, it offers easy access to Salzburg's attractions while providing a peaceful retreat.

- **Price Range**: €90 - €170 per night.
- **Address**: Brunnauerstraße 3, 5020 Salzburg, Austria.
- **Contact**: +43 662 87 28 25
- **Website**: www.hotel-brunnauer.at

4. The Mozart Hotel

Overview: This boutique hotel is dedicated to the famous composer Wolfgang Amadeus Mozart, celebrating his life and music throughout its decor. The hotel is located in the city center and offers modern amenities while reflecting Salzburg's musical heritage. The staff is known for its friendliness and willingness to help guests explore the city.

- **Price Range**: €100 - €180 per night.
- **Address**: Makartplatz 5, 5020 Salzburg, Austria.
- **Contact**: +43 662 84 11 40
- **Website**: www.hotelmozart.com

5. Hotel Villa Carlton

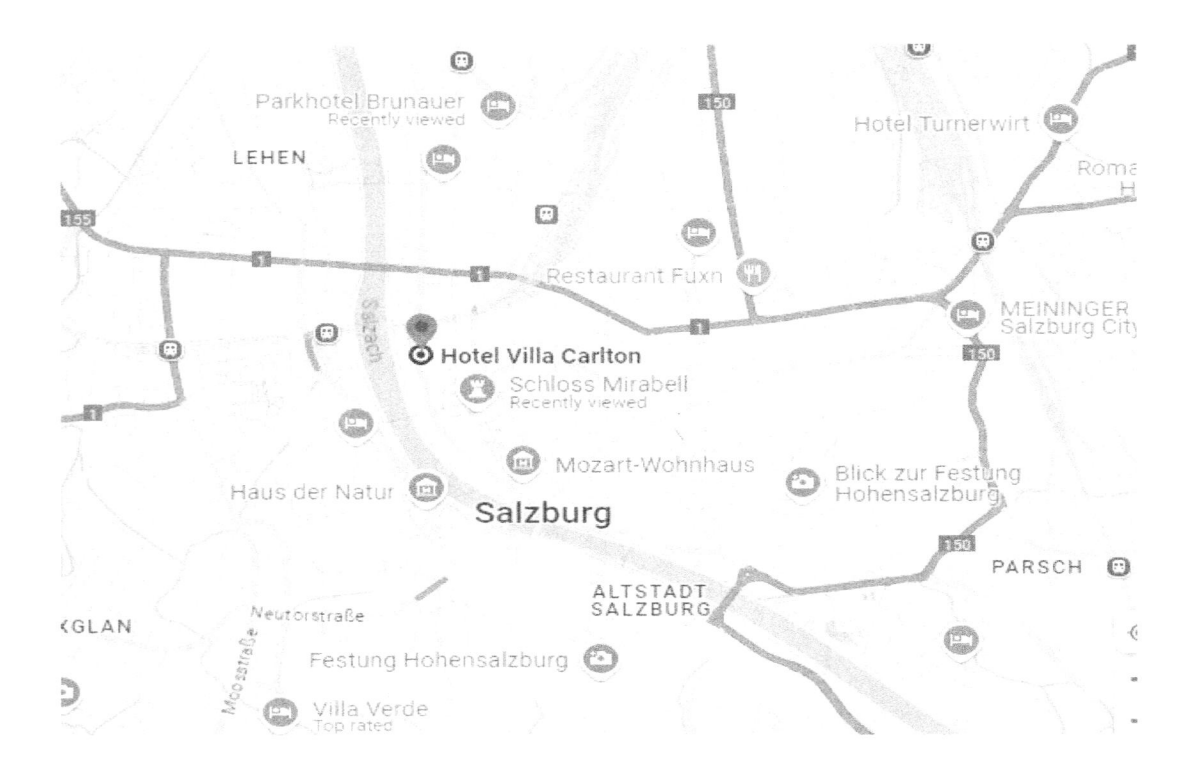

Overview: Hotel Villa Carlton is a stylish boutique hotel that combines contemporary design with traditional Austrian hospitality. Located close to the city center, the hotel features comfortable rooms, a beautiful terrace, and a wellness area. The hotel's architecture and decor are inspired by the history of Salzburg, providing a unique atmosphere.

- **Price Range**: €150 - €250 per night.
- **Address**: Elisabethstraße 1, 5020 Salzburg, Austria.
- **Contact**: +43 662 87 80 00
- **Website**: www.villacarlton.at

6. Hotel Elefant

Overview: Nestled in the Old Town, Hotel Elefant is a boutique hotel known for its unique charm and history. The hotel features individually decorated rooms, a cozy bar, and a delightful courtyard. Its prime location makes it easy to explore the nearby attractions.

- **Price Range**: €120 - €200 per night.
- **Address**: Sigmund-Haffner-Gasse 4, 5020 Salzburg, Austria.
- **Contact**: +43 662 84 28 34
- **Website**: www.hotelelefant.at

7. Hotel Auersperg

Overview: Hotel Auersperg is a stylish boutique hotel with a focus on sustainability and comfort. It features modern design, a beautiful garden, and a wellness area for relaxation. Located near the city center, the hotel is a perfect base for exploring Salzburg.

- **Price Range**: €140 - €250 per night.
- **Address**: Auerspergstraße 61, 5020 Salzburg, Austria.
- **Contact**: +43 662 88 56 56
- **Website**: www.auersperg.at

8. Schloss Mönchstein Hotel

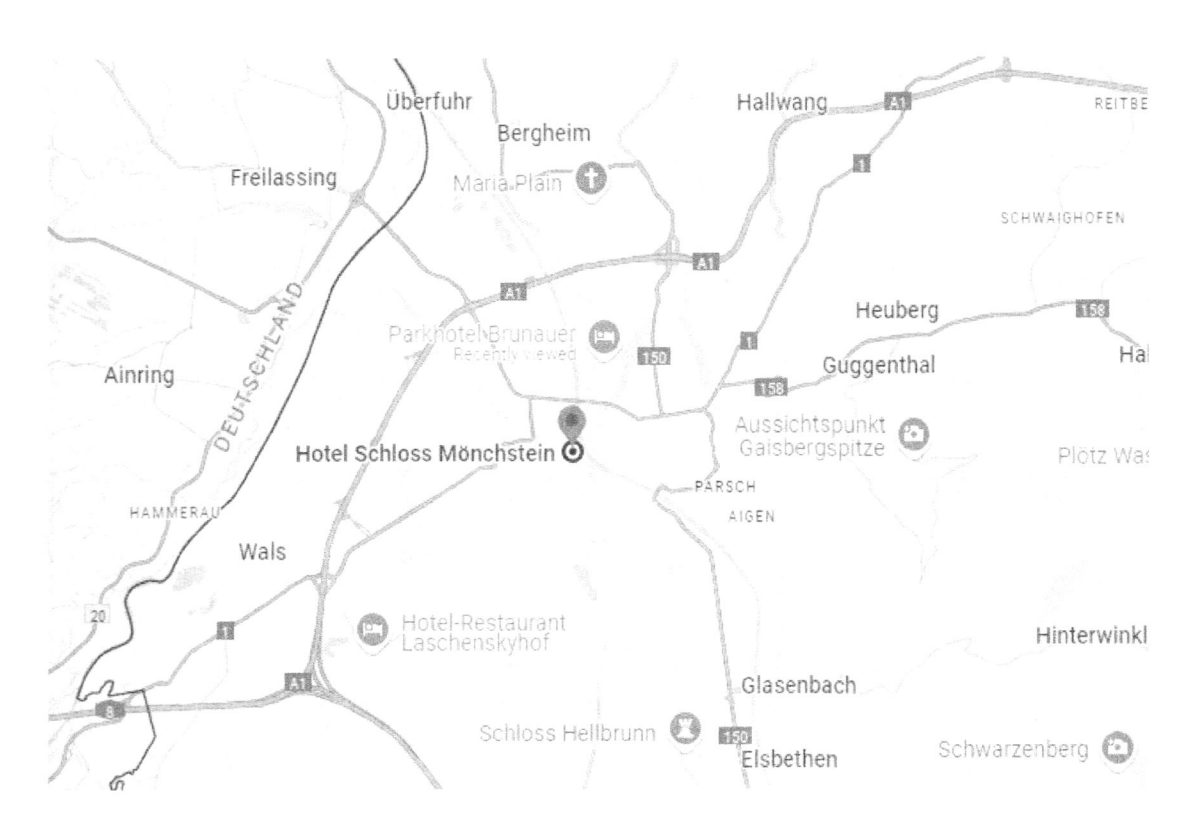

Overview: Set in a historic castle on a hill overlooking Salzburg, Schloss Mönchstein offers a truly unique experience. This luxurious hotel features beautifully appointed rooms, fine dining, and stunning views of the city and mountains. It's a great option for those looking for a romantic getaway or a special occasion.

- **Price Range**: €300 - €600 per night.
- **Address**: Mönchsteinstraße 3, 5020 Salzburg, Austria.
- **Contact**: +43 662 84 40 40
- **Website**: www.schloss-moenchstein.com

9. Hotel Stadtkrug

Overview: Located in the historic part of Salzburg, Hotel Stadtkrug offers a blend of traditional and modern design. The hotel is known for its cozy rooms and friendly service. It's a great base for exploring the city's attractions, with easy access to public transport.

- **Price Range**: €100 - €180 per night.
- **Address**: Linzergasse 20, 5020 Salzburg, Austria.
- **Contact**: +43 662 87 29 80
- **Website**: www.stadtkrug.at

Conclusion

Staying in a boutique hotel or unique accommodation can enhance your experience in Salzburg, offering a chance to enjoy the city in a more personalized way. With options ranging from historic hotels to stylish modern stays, you can find the perfect place that reflects your style and needs. Whether you're looking for luxury, charm, or a memorable atmosphere, these unique accommodations will make your visit to Salzburg even more special.

5.3 Tips for Booking

Booking accommodation for your trip to Salzburg can be exciting, but it's also important to make informed decisions to ensure a smooth and enjoyable experience. Here are some essential tips to help you find the best places to stay in Salzburg, whether you're looking for luxury, a boutique experience, or budget-friendly options.

1. Plan Ahead

Overview: Salzburg is a popular travel destination, especially during peak seasons (spring, summer, and the Christmas markets). Booking your accommodation in advance can help you secure the best options and prices. Aim to book at least two to three months before your travel dates, especially if you plan to visit during a busy period or if you have specific hotels in mind.

2. Set a Budget

Overview: Establish a clear budget for your accommodation before you start searching. Consider all potential expenses, including taxes and fees, which can vary significantly between hotels and hostels. This will help narrow down your options and prevent overspending.

3. Consider Location

Overview: The location of your accommodation is crucial to making the most of your trip. Staying in or near the Old Town (Altstadt) will give you easy access to major attractions, restaurants, and public transport. If you prefer a quieter environment, consider accommodations a bit farther from the tourist areas but still within walking distance or close to public transport.

4. Read Reviews

Overview: Before booking, read reviews from other travelers on platforms like TripAdvisor, Google, or Booking.com. Look for feedback about cleanliness, service, location, and amenities. Reviews can provide valuable insights that help you choose the right place for your needs.

5. Check Amenities

Overview: Different hotels and hostels offer various amenities that can enhance your stay. Consider what is important for you, such as free Wi-Fi, breakfast options, laundry facilities, or pet-friendly policies. Checking for specific amenities will ensure you choose a place that meets your needs.

6. Look for Deals and Discounts

Overview: Many hotels offer special deals, discounts, or packages, especially during the off-peak season. Check hotel websites and booking platforms for any promotions. Consider joining loyalty programs or using travel reward points if you frequently stay in hotels.

7. Flexibility with Dates

Overview: If your travel dates are flexible, consider adjusting them to find better rates. Mid-week stays are often cheaper than weekends, and traveling during the shoulder season (late autumn or early spring) can help you save money while avoiding the crowds.

8. Book Directly

Overview: Whenever possible, book directly through the hotel's website. Direct bookings often come with better rates, special perks, or flexible cancellation policies. Additionally, you may find that hotels prioritize direct bookings, providing better service upon arrival.

9. Understand Cancellation Policies

Overview: Before finalizing your booking, make sure to read and understand the cancellation policies. Some accommodations offer flexible cancellation options, while others may have stricter terms. Knowing this information can save you from unexpected fees if your plans change.

10. Use Trusted Booking Platforms

Overview: When booking online, use reputable platforms like Booking.com, Expedia, or Airbnb. These sites provide customer support and detailed listings, helping you avoid scams or misleading information.

11. Consider Alternative Accommodations

Overview: Don't limit your search to traditional hotels. Consider alternative accommodations like guesthouses, hostels, or vacation rentals. These options can offer a unique experience and often come at a lower price.

12. Contact the Hotel Directly

Overview: If you have specific requests (like late check-in or special needs), don't hesitate to contact the hotel directly. Speaking with staff can help clarify any questions you have and ensure your stay meets your expectations.

Conclusion

Booking accommodation in Salzburg can be a smooth process if you take the time to plan and consider your options. By following these tips, you can find the perfect place to stay that suits your budget, preferences, and needs. Enjoy your trip to this beautiful city, and make the most of your unique accommodation experience!

Seasonal Events and Festivals

6.1 Overview of Annual Festivals

Salzburg is renowned for its rich cultural heritage and vibrant traditions, which come to life through various annual festivals and events. Each year, the city hosts a range of festivities that celebrate music, art, food, and local customs, drawing both locals and tourists alike. Here's a comprehensive overview of the major annual festivals in Salzburg, highlighting their unique features and significance.

1. Salzburg Festival (Salzburger Festspiele)

When: Late July to late August

Overview: The Salzburg Festival is one of the most prestigious and celebrated music festivals in the world. Founded in 1920, it attracts top musicians, conductors, and performers from around the globe. The festival primarily features operas, concerts, and theatrical performances, with many events held in iconic venues such as the Salzburg Festival Hall and the Grosses Festspielhaus. The festival showcases works by famous composers, including Mozart, and often includes premieres of new works.

Highlights:

- Daily performances, including operas, classical concerts, and drama.
- Special events and open-air performances in beautiful settings, such as Mirabell Palace Gardens.
- The atmosphere is filled with excitement as both locals and visitors immerse themselves in high-quality art and culture.

2. Advent and Christmas Markets

When: Late November to December 24

Overview: Salzburg's Advent season is magical, with festive decorations illuminating the city and the scent of roasted chestnuts filling the air. The Christmas markets (Weihnachtsmärkte) are a highlight, offering handmade crafts, local delicacies, The most famous market is held in the Cathedral Square (Domplatz), providing a picturesque backdrop against the stunning Salzburg Cathedral.

Highlights:

- Traditional music performances and carol singing.
- Opportunities to purchase unique gifts, ornaments, and artisanal foods.
- Special activities for children, including visits from Santa Claus.

3. Salzburg Easter Festival (Salzburger Osterfestspiele)

When: Easter weekend (dates vary each year)

Overview: The Salzburg Easter Festival is a celebration of classical music and the Easter holiday, founded in 1967 by conductor Herbert von Karajan. The festival features a series of concerts, operas, and sacred music performances, focusing on works by Bach, Handel, and other classical composers. The festival draws talented musicians from around the world and offers a spiritually uplifting experience.

Highlights:

- Performances in stunning venues, including St. Peter's Church.
- A mix of traditional and contemporary classical music.
- Family-friendly events and activities to celebrate the Easter spirit.

4. Salzburg Mozart Week (Mozartwoche)

When: January 27 - February 5

Overview: Mozart Week celebrates the life and works of Salzburg's most famous son, Wolfgang Amadeus Mozart. This annual festival coincides with Mozart's birthday on January 27 and features a variety of concerts, including chamber music, operas, and symphonies performed by renowned artists and ensembles. The week highlights both well-known compositions and lesser-known works.

Highlights:

- Performances in venues closely associated with Mozart, such as his birthplace and the Mozarteum.
- Special lectures and discussions about Mozart's life and influence.
- Interactive events, including workshops and masterclasses for music enthusiasts.

5. Salzburg Film Festival (Salzburg International Festival)

When: Late September to early October

Overview: This festival is a celebration of cinema that showcases both national and international films. The Salzburg Film Festival focuses on promoting new filmmakers and innovative films, providing a platform for discussions and networking within the film industry. It features various genres, including documentaries, feature films, and shorts.

Highlights:

- Screenings of films in unique venues across the city, including historical sites and outdoor settings.
- Opportunities to meet filmmakers and participate in Q&A sessions.
- Awards and recognitions for outstanding films and filmmakers.

6. Salzburg World of Music (Salzburger Musiktage)

When: Various dates throughout the year

Overview: The Salzburg World of Music is a series of events celebrating diverse musical genres, including classical, jazz, folk, and world music. This festival aims to promote the city's rich musical heritage while introducing contemporary and global sounds to the audience.

Highlights:

- Concerts held in various venues, from churches to outdoor stages.
- Workshops and educational programs for aspiring musicians and music lovers.
- A focus on cultural exchange and collaboration between local and international artists.

Highlights:

- Tasting events with local food .
- Interactive cooking classes and workshops led by renowned chefs.
- Opportunities to meet local producers and learn about their craft.

Conclusion

Salzburg's annual festivals are a vibrant reflection of the city's rich cultural heritage and artistic spirit. From world-class music festivals to festive holiday markets, each event offers visitors a chance to experience the local traditions, music, and gastronomy that make Salzburg a truly special destination.

6.2 Winter Holiday Celebrations

Winter in Salzburg transforms the city into a stunning wonderland filled with festive cheer, lights, and traditions. The air is crisp, and the atmosphere is charged with excitement as locals and visitors come together to celebrate the holiday season. Here's a comprehensive overview of the winter holiday celebrations in Salzburg, focusing on key events and traditions that make this time of year special.

1. Advent Season

Overview: The Advent season marks the countdown to Christmas, and Salzburg embraces this time with warmth and joy. From late November until Christmas Eve, the city is adorned with beautiful decorations, and the spirit of the holidays can be felt everywhere.

Highlights:

- **Advent Markets**: Several Christmas markets pop up throughout the city, the most famous being the market in the Cathedral Square (Domplatz). Here, you can find a variety of handmade crafts, decorations, and delicious seasonal treats, such as gingerbread (Lebkuchen) and roasted chestnuts.
- **Traditional Decorations**: Streets and squares are decorated with twinkling lights, wreaths, and Christmas trees, creating a magical atmosphere. Many shops also display festive window decorations, making shopping a delightful experience.
- **Advent Music**: The sounds of carols and traditional Advent music fill the air, with choirs performing in various locations, including churches and public squares. This musical ambiance adds to the festive spirit and invites people to gather and celebrate.

2. Christmas Markets (Weihnachtsmärkte)

Overview: Salzburg's Christmas markets are a highlight of the winter season, attracting thousands of visitors each year. Each market has its own unique charm, but all share a focus on local crafts, festive food, and a joyful atmosphere.

Key Markets:

- **Salzburg Christkindlmarkt**: Located in the historic Cathedral Square, this market is the oldest in the city, dating back to 1491. Visitors can browse over 100 stalls selling handcrafted gifts, ornaments, and delicious treats.
- **Mirabell Christmas Market**: Set in the beautiful Mirabell Gardens, this market offers a more relaxed atmosphere with stunning views of Hohensalzburg Fortress. It features local artisans showcasing their crafts and a cozy ambiance perfect for families.
- **Hellbrunn Christmas Market**: This enchanting market is held in the grounds of Hellbrunn Palace and is known for its picturesque setting and charming decorations. Visitors can enjoy the Christmas atmosphere while exploring the palace's beautiful gardens.

3. Christmas Eve (Heiligabend)

Overview: In Austria, Christmas Eve is considered the most important day of the festive season. Families gather for special meals and celebrations, and many traditions are observed.

Highlights:

- **Christmas Dinner**: Families often enjoy a festive meal together, which may include dishes like roast goose, carp, or various traditional Austrian pastries.
- **Gift Giving**: Gifts are exchanged on Christmas Eve rather than Christmas Day. Children eagerly await the arrival of the Christkind, a figure resembling the Christmas angel, who delivers presents.
- **Church Services**: Many locals attend evening church services, known as "Christmette," where they celebrate the birth of Jesus. Churches are beautifully decorated, and the services often feature festive music and candlelight.

4. Christmas Day (Erster Feiertag)

Overview: Christmas Day is a time for relaxation and spending quality time with family and friends. Many people enjoy a leisurely breakfast and continue the celebrations from the previous night.

Highlights:

- **Christmas Brunch**: Families often gather for a festive brunch that includes treats like stollen (a fruitcake) and various pastries. This meal is a more relaxed affair after the busy Christmas Eve.
- **Family Activities**: Outdoor activities such as ice skating or sledding are popular during the holiday season, allowing families to enjoy the winter scenery together.

5. New Year's Eve (Silvester)

Overview: The transition to the new year is celebrated with much enthusiasm in Salzburg. New Year's Eve, known as Silvester, is marked by various festivities throughout the city.

Highlights:

- **Public Celebrations**: Many people gather in the Old Town and other public squares to celebrate with fireworks, music, and dancing. The atmosphere is lively, with a sense of excitement and anticipation for the coming year.
- **Fireworks Display**: A spectacular fireworks show illuminates the sky, providing a breathtaking view from various vantage points throughout the city. The best spots to enjoy the display include the banks of the Salzach River and the area near Hohensalzburg Fortress.

- **Traditions**: Austrians often enjoy a traditional New Year's Eve meal that may include a special cake called "Neujahrskrapfen" (a jelly-filled doughnut)
- **6. Three Kings Day (Heilige Drei Könige)**

When: January 6

Overview: The celebration of Three Kings Day marks the end of the Christmas season and is an important holiday in Austria. It commemorates the visit of the Magi to the baby Jesus and is celebrated with various customs and festivities.

Highlights:

- **Processions**: In many towns and cities, processions featuring people dressed as the Three Wise Men take place. These processions often include music and traditional costumes, creating a festive atmosphere.
- **Blessing of Homes**: It is common for families to have their homes blessed on this day. The Three Kings are represented by chalk inscriptions on doorways, a tradition believed to bring blessings and protection for the coming year.
- **Traditional Treats**: Special pastries called "Dreikönigskuchen" (Three Kings cake) are enjoyed during this time. These cakes often contain hidden figurines, and the person who finds the figurine is believed to have good luck for the year ahead.

Conclusion

Winter holiday celebrations in Salzburg offer a unique blend of tradition, music, and joy. The city comes alive with festive markets, beautiful decorations, and heartwarming traditions that reflect the rich cultural heritage of Austria. Whether you're exploring the magical Christmas markets, enjoying festive meals with locals, or experiencing the excitement of New Year's Eve, Salzburg in winter is a truly enchanting destination that leaves a lasting impression on all who visit.

6.3 Summer Events and Outdoor Activities

Summer in Salzburg is a vibrant time filled with various events, festivals, and outdoor activities that celebrate the beauty of the season. With its stunning landscapes, historic architecture, and lively atmosphere, the city offers many opportunities for both locals and visitors to enjoy the warm weather. Here's a comprehensive overview of the summer events and outdoor activities you can experience in Salzburg.

1. Salzburg Festival (Salzburger Festspiele)

When: Late July to late August

Overview: As previously mentioned, the Salzburg Festival is a highlight of the summer cultural calendar. It's a prestigious festival featuring world-class performances in opera, classical music, and theater. Visitors can enjoy a variety of events in stunning venues across the city, including the famous Festspielhaus and the historic Hohensalzburg Fortress.

Highlights:

- **Open-Air Performances**: Some performances may take place outdoors, allowing audiences to enjoy the summer evenings while experiencing exceptional art.
- **Special Events**: The festival often hosts lectures, discussions, and masterclasses that provide deeper insights into the performances and the works being showcased.
- **Young Artist Programs**: The festival also promotes emerging talents, offering a platform for young artists to showcase their skills, making it an exciting time to witness fresh interpretations of classic works.

2. Salzburger Volksfest

When: Mid-August

Overview: The Salzburger Volksfest is a lively folk festival that celebrates the region's traditions and culture. This festival is a perfect blend of music, food, and entertainment, attracting thousands of visitors each year.

Highlights:

- **Traditional Music and Dance**: Enjoy performances by local folk bands, choirs, and dance groups. Traditional Austrian dances and music create a festive atmosphere that encourages audience participation.
- **Culinary Delights**: Food stalls offer a range of local specialties, including sausages, pretzels, and sweet treats. Don't miss the chance to try traditional dishes while enjoying the lively ambiance.
- **Amusement Rides**: The festival features various amusement rides and games, making it a fun outing for families and visitors of all ages.

3. Outdoor Concerts and Festivals

Overview: Throughout the summer, Salzburg hosts a variety of outdoor concerts and music festivals, showcasing different genres and attracting both local and international artists. These events often take place in beautiful outdoor settings, allowing visitors to enjoy music surrounded by stunning landscapes.

Highlights:

- **Jazz and Blues Festivals**: These festivals feature live performances from talented musicians in various parks and public spaces. Enjoy a laid-back atmosphere as you listen to smooth jazz or upbeat blues while soaking up the sun.
- **Classical Music in the Park**: Many parks host classical music concerts, allowing you to experience beautiful compositions while relaxing outdoors. Bring a picnic blanket, grab some snacks, and enjoy an evening of music under the stars.
- **World Music Festival**: This festival celebrates global music traditions, featuring performances from artists around the world. It's a fantastic opportunity to explore different cultures through music and dance.

4. Hiking and Nature Activities

Overview: Salzburg is surrounded by breathtaking natural beauty, making it an ideal destination for outdoor enthusiasts. Summer is the perfect time to explore the many hiking trails and enjoy various nature activities in the nearby mountains and lakes.

Highlights:

- **Hiking Trails**: Numerous hiking trails cater to all skill levels, from leisurely walks to challenging hikes. The nearby Untersberg mountain offers stunning views and well-marked trails for a rewarding outdoor experience.
- **Lakes and Swimming**: Visit the beautiful lakes around Salzburg, such as Wolfgangsee or Fuschlsee, for swimming, sunbathing, and water sports. Many lakes have designated swimming areas, picnic spots, and facilities for renting boats or paddleboards.
- **Cycling**: The city and surrounding areas offer a network of cycling paths, making it easy to explore the region on two wheels. Rent a bike and take a leisurely ride along the Salzach River or venture into the countryside for scenic views.

5. Salzburg's Parks and Gardens

Overview: Summer is an excellent time to enjoy Salzburg's beautiful parks and gardens. These green spaces offer a relaxing environment for picnics, leisurely walks, and outdoor activities.

Highlights:

- **Mirabell Gardens**: Famous for its stunning floral displays, the Mirabell Gardens is a popular spot for visitors. Take a stroll through the meticulously landscaped gardens and enjoy the views of Hohensalzburg Fortress.
- **Hellbrunn Palace Gardens**: The gardens surrounding Hellbrunn Palace are perfect for exploring during the summer. Discover the famous trick fountains, beautiful flower beds, and shaded pathways that make for a lovely day out.

- **Dult Fair**: Held in August, the Dult Fair is a local event that takes place in the parks of Salzburg. It features local crafts, food stalls, and entertainment, making it a great way to experience the community's spirit.

6. Cultural Events and Exhibitions

Overview: Summer is a vibrant time for cultural events in Salzburg, including art exhibitions, theater performances, and film screenings. Various galleries and theaters host special events that showcase local talent and international artists.

Highlights:

- **Art in the Park**: Many parks host temporary art installations and exhibitions during the summer months, providing a unique way to engage with contemporary art in an outdoor setting.
- **Theater Performances**: Local theaters may host outdoor performances, offering a variety of plays and shows that take advantage of the beautiful summer evenings.
- **Film Festivals**: Open-air film screenings are popular during the summer, providing a chance to watch classic films or contemporary cinema in a charming outdoor setting.

Conclusion

Summer in Salzburg is filled with vibrant events and outdoor activities that celebrate the city's culture, traditions, and natural beauty. From the prestigious Salzburg Festival to lively folk celebrations, visitors can immerse themselves in the local atmosphere while enjoying the great outdoors. Whether you're hiking in the nearby mountains, relaxing by a lake, or attending a concert in the park, summer in Salzburg offers something for everyone to enjoy!

Day Trips and Excursions

7.1 Exploring the Surrounding Region

Salzburg is not just a city rich in history and culture; it also serves as a gateway to some of Austria's most stunning natural landscapes and charming towns. The region surrounding Salzburg offers a plethora of opportunities for day trips and excursions, allowing visitors to experience the beauty of the Alps, picturesque lakes, and enchanting villages. Here's a comprehensive guide to some of the best places to explore just a short journey from Salzburg.

1. Hallstatt

Distance from Salzburg: About 1 hour and 15 minutes by car or 2 hours by train.

Overview: Hallstatt is a UNESCO World Heritage Site known for its breathtaking lakeside setting and charming architecture. The village, with its narrow streets and pastel-colored houses, is one of Austria's most photographed locations.

Highlights:

- **Hallstatt Lake**: Enjoy a leisurely boat ride on Hallstatt Lake, where you can take in the stunning views of the surrounding mountains and the quaint village.
- **Salt Mines**: Visit the historic salt mines, which have been in operation for thousands of years. Guided tours provide insights into the mining process and the region's history. Don't miss the chance to ride the funicular for a panoramic view of Hallstatt.
- **Skywalk**: For an unforgettable view, hike up to the Hallstatt Skywalk, which offers breathtaking views of the village and the lake below.

Tips: Arrive early in the morning or later in the afternoon to avoid the large tourist crowds that flock to Hallstatt during peak hours.

2. Wolfgangsee (Lake Wolfgang)

Distance from Salzburg: Approximately 30 minutes by car or 1 hour by public transport.

Overview: Lake Wolfgang is a stunning alpine lake surrounded by mountains and charming towns, including St. Wolfgang and Strobl. It's an excellent destination for relaxation and outdoor activities.

Highlights:

- **Boating and Swimming**: Rent a boat or swim in the crystal-clear waters of the lake. There are designated swimming areas with facilities, perfect for a refreshing dip on a hot summer day.
- **Hiking and Biking**: Numerous trails surround the lake, catering to hikers and cyclists of all skill levels. The trail around the lake offers beautiful views and plenty of spots to stop for a picnic.
- **St. Wolfgang**: Visit the charming town of St. Wolfgang, known for its beautiful church and vibrant local shops. Don't miss trying the famous "Wolfgangsee Fish" at a lakeside restaurant.

Tips: The best time to visit is during the summer months when the weather is warm, and outdoor activities are in full swing.

3. Berchtesgaden National Park

Distance from Salzburg: About 30 minutes by car.

Overview: This stunning national park is located just across the border in Germany and is home to the iconic Watzmann mountain and beautiful alpine landscapes. It's a paradise for nature lovers and outdoor enthusiasts.

Highlights:

- **Konigssee**: Take a boat ride on Königssee, a crystal-clear lake surrounded by towering mountains. The ride to the famous St. Bartholomew's Church is a highlight, as the views are breathtaking.
- **Hiking Trails**: Explore a variety of hiking trails ranging from easy walks to more challenging hikes. The path to the Röthbach Waterfall, the highest waterfall in Germany, is a must for adventure seekers.
- **Eagle's Nest**: Visit the historical site known as the Eagle's Nest (Kehlsteinhaus), which offers stunning panoramic views of the Alps. The site is accessible via a bus and elevator from the parking area.

Tips: Bring a camera for the stunning views and wear sturdy hiking shoes if you plan to explore the trails.

4. Salzburg's Salt Mines (Salzbergwerk)

Distance from Salzburg: About 30 minutes by car to Bad Dürrnberg.

Overview: The salt mines near Salzburg offer a unique glimpse into the region's mining history. The mines have been in operation for over 2,500 years and are among the oldest in the world.

Highlights:

- **Guided Tours**: Join a guided tour of the salt mines, where you'll learn about the history and importance of salt mining in Salzburg's economy. The tour includes funicular rides, slides, and an underground lake.
- **Miner's Museum**: Explore the Miner's Museum to learn more about the life of miners and the history of salt extraction in the area.

Tips: Dress warmly, as the temperature inside the mines can be much cooler than outside.

5. Innsbruck

Distance from Salzburg: Approximately 1 hour and 50 minutes by car or 2 hours by train.

Overview: Innsbruck is the capital of Tyrol and is nestled in the heart of the Alps. Known for its beautiful architecture and outdoor sports, it's a great place for a day trip.

Highlights:

- **Golden Roof**: Visit the famous Golden Roof (Goldenes Dachl), a landmark adorned with 2,657 fire-gilded copper tiles, located in the heart of Innsbruck's Old Town.
- **Swarovski Crystal Worlds**: Explore the nearby Swarovski Crystal Worlds (Swarovski Kristallwelten) in Wattens, a fascinating place that showcases the beauty of crystals in art and design.
- **Nordkette Mountains**: Take a cable car ride up to the Nordkette mountain range for hiking, mountain biking, or simply enjoying the stunning views of the Innsbruck valley.

Tips: Innsbruck can be busy, especially in the summer, so consider visiting during the week to enjoy a more relaxed experience.

6. Golling Waterfall (Gollinger Wasserfall)

Distance from Salzburg: About 30 minutes by car.

Overview: Golling Waterfall is a stunning natural attraction located near the town of Golling. This picturesque waterfall cascades down rocks into a beautiful pool, creating a peaceful atmosphere.

Highlights:

- **Hiking Trail**: The short hike to the waterfall is easy and family-friendly, with well-marked paths that lead through lush forest and alongside the river.
- **Photography**: The waterfall offers great photo opportunities, especially during sunny days when rainbows can form in the mist.

Tips: Bring a picnic to enjoy at one of the scenic spots near the waterfall.

Conclusion

Exploring the surrounding region of Salzburg opens up a world of natural beauty, history, and culture. Whether you're visiting charming villages, enjoying outdoor adventures, or immersing yourself in Austria's rich heritage, there are countless day trips and excursions that enhance your experience in this enchanting part of the world. With so much to see and do just a short distance from the city, your time in Salzburg will be filled with unforgettable memories and experiences!

7.2 Popular Day Trip Destinations

Salzburg is a fantastic base for exploring some of the most beautiful and interesting destinations in Austria and beyond. Whether you're seeking stunning natural landscapes, charming towns, or historical sites, there are plenty of popular day trip options that are easily accessible from the city. Here are some top recommendations:

1. Cesky Krumlov, Czech Republic

Distance from Salzburg: Approximately 2.5 hours by car or bus.

Overview: This picturesque town, a UNESCO World Heritage Site, is famous for its stunning medieval architecture and the well-preserved Cesky Krumlov Castle, which towers over the Vltava River.

Highlights:

- **Cesky Krumlov Castle**: Explore the expansive castle complex, which features beautiful gardens and offers panoramic views of the town and river.
- **Old Town**: Wander the cobbled streets of the Old Town, filled with colorful buildings, quaint shops, and local cafés.
- **River Activities**: In summer, enjoy canoeing or kayaking on the Vltava River, or relax by the riverside with a picnic.

Tips: Consider visiting during weekdays to avoid the large tourist crowds that typically gather on weekends.

2. The Salzkammergut Region

Distance from Salzburg: About 30 minutes to 1 hour, depending on the destination.

Overview: The Salzkammergut is a stunning region known for its beautiful lakes and mountains. It offers numerous outdoor activities and picturesque villages.

Popular Lakes:

- **Wolfgangsee**: A popular lake for swimming, sailing, and hiking, with beautiful towns like St. Wolfgang and Strobl surrounding it.
- **Fuschlsee**: A smaller, tranquil lake perfect for swimming and picnicking, known for its clear waters.
- **Attersee**: One of the largest lakes in Austria, ideal for water sports, fishing, and hiking in the surrounding mountains.

Highlights:

- **Scenic Drives**: Enjoy scenic drives through the region, stopping at charming villages and lakeside spots.
- **Hiking Trails**: Numerous trails range from easy lakeside walks to challenging mountain hikes with breathtaking views.

Tips: Bring your swimwear if you plan to swim in the lakes during the warmer months.

3. Berchtesgaden, Germany

Distance from Salzburg: About 30 minutes by car.

Overview: Located just over the border in Germany, Berchtesgaden is a beautiful town set against the backdrop of the Bavarian Alps. It's known for its stunning natural beauty and outdoor activities.

Highlights:

- **Konigssee**: Visit the pristine Königssee lake, where you can take a boat trip to St. Bartholomew's Church. The surrounding mountains provide a breathtaking backdrop.
- **Eagle's Nest**: Take a bus and elevator ride up to the Eagle's Nest (Kehlsteinhaus), a historical site offering incredible views of the Alps.
- **Hiking**: The area has numerous hiking trails, catering to all levels, with stunning vistas and natural beauty.

Tips: Check the weather before your trip, as conditions in the mountains can change quickly.

4. Passau

Distance from Salzburg: Approximately 1.5 hours by car or train.

Overview: Passau, known as the "City of Three Rivers," is located at the confluence of the Danube, Inn, and Ilz rivers. It's famous for its baroque architecture and picturesque old town.

Highlights:

- **St. Stephen's Cathedral**: Visit this impressive cathedral, which houses one of the largest pipe organs in the world.
- **Old Town**: Stroll through the charming streets of the Old Town, lined with colorful buildings and cafés.
- **River Cruises**: Consider taking a river cruise to enjoy the scenic beauty of the area from the water.

Tips: Check the schedule for local events or festivals that may be happening during your visit for an enriched experience.

5. Innsbruck

Distance from Salzburg: Approximately 1 hour and 50 minutes by car or 2 hours by train.

Overview: The capital of Tyrol, Innsbruck is famous for its historical sites and stunning mountain scenery, making it a great day trip destination.

Highlights:

- **Golden Roof**: Explore this iconic landmark in the Old Town, adorned with 2,657 gilded tiles.
- **Nordkette Mountain Range**: Take a cable car up to the Nordkette for hiking, skiing (in winter), or simply to enjoy the panoramic views of the city below.
- **Swarovski Crystal Worlds**: Visit the nearby Swarovski Crystal Worlds for a unique experience filled with art, design, and dazzling crystals.

Tips: Consider a day trip that includes both the city sights and a trip to the mountains for a well-rounded experience.

6. Melk Abbey

Distance from Salzburg: About 1.5 hours by car.

Overview: Melk Abbey is a magnificent Benedictine monastery overlooking the Danube River. It's renowned for its baroque architecture and beautiful gardens.

Highlights:

- **Abbey Tour**: Take a guided tour of the abbey to learn about its history and admire the stunning architecture, including the impressive library and church.
- **Gardens**: Walk through the abbey gardens, offering beautiful views of the Danube and the surrounding landscape.
- **Danube River**: Consider taking a boat ride along the Danube to enjoy the scenic beauty of the river and surrounding countryside.

Tips: Check the abbey's opening hours in advance, as they may vary throughout the year.

7. Grossglockner High Alpine Road

Distance from Salzburg: About 1.5 hours by car.

Overview: The Grossglockner High Alpine Road is one of the most scenic drives in Austria, leading you through breathtaking mountain landscapes to the foot of Austria's highest peak, Grossglockner.

Highlights:

- **Panoramic Views**: Enjoy stunning views of the Grossglockner and the Pasterze Glacier along the road, with multiple viewing platforms.
- **Hiking**: There are several hiking trails accessible from the road, offering a chance to explore the alpine flora and fauna.
- **Visitor Center**: Stop at the Kaiser Franz Josefs Höhe Visitor Center to learn more about the region's natural history and enjoy the views from their observation deck.

Tips: The road is typically open from May to October, depending on weather conditions. Check the official website for updates before your visit.

Conclusion

Exploring the popular day trip destinations around Salzburg offers a wonderful opportunity to experience the beauty and diversity of Austria and its neighboring regions. From charming towns and historic sites to stunning natural landscapes, there's something for everyone. Whether you're looking to relax by a lake, hike in the mountains, or immerse yourself in history, these day trips will enrich your visit to Salzburg and create lasting memories!

7.3 Nature and Outdoor Activities

Salzburg is not just a city filled with history and culture; it is also surrounded by stunning natural landscapes that make it a haven for outdoor enthusiasts. Whether you're interested in hiking, skiing, biking, or simply enjoying nature, there's an abundance of activities for everyone. This section explores the best ways to experience the great outdoors in and around Salzburg.

1. Hiking

Hiking is one of the most popular outdoor activities in Salzburg, thanks to its picturesque scenery and well-maintained trails. From leisurely walks to challenging mountain hikes, there are options for all levels of hikers.

1.1. Local Trails

- **Untersberg Mountain**: Located just a short drive from the city, Untersberg is a must-visit for hikers. The trail to the summit offers breathtaking views of the Alps and the city below. It takes about 3-4 hours to reach the top, but you can also take a cable car partway up, making it easier for families and those looking for a less strenuous experience.
- **Gaisberg Mountain**: Gaisberg is another local favorite, known for its beautiful panoramic views of Salzburg. The hike typically takes 2-3 hours, and the area is also popular for mountain biking.
- **Hellbrunner Allee**: This scenic walking path runs from Hellbrunn Palace to the outskirts of the city. It's an easy stroll that takes about 1-2 hours, featuring lovely gardens and views of the Alps along the way.

1.2. Longer Hikes

- **The Salzburger Almenweg**: This long-distance trail covers about 350 kilometers (217 miles) through the Salzburger Land region. It is divided into stages, so you can choose shorter sections for day hikes. Hikers will encounter stunning alpine landscapes, traditional huts, and diverse wildlife.
- **Glockner Circuit**: For those looking for a multi-day hiking experience, the Glockner Circuit takes you around Grossglockner, Austria's highest mountain. This trek usually spans 5-6 days, with accommodation options along the route.

2. Biking

Biking is another excellent way to explore the stunning landscapes surrounding Salzburg. Numerous cycling routes cater to various skill levels, from easy family-friendly paths to challenging mountain trails.

2.1. Bike Rentals

You can easily rent bicycles in Salzburg from several local shops that offer mountain bikes, city bikes, and e-bikes for those who need a little assistance on uphill climbs. Popular rental locations include:

- **Bike-Point Salzburg**: Conveniently located near the city center, they provide a wide range of bike options. Website: bikepoint-salzburg.at
- **Radhaus Salzburg**: Another good choice, with a variety of bikes available for different needs. Website: radhaus-salzburg.at

2.2. Cycling Routes

- **The Salzach River Cycle Path**: This scenic route follows the Salzach River and extends approximately 50 kilometers (31 miles) from Salzburg to the Austrian-German border. It's a flat, well-maintained path suitable for cyclists of all levels. Enjoy the peaceful river views and charming countryside along the way.
- **The Enns Cycle Path**: For a longer biking adventure, consider this route that takes you from the Dachstein mountain region to Enns. The trail is about 250 kilometers (155 miles) long and features beautiful views throughout the ride.
- **Mountain Biking Trails**: The areas surrounding Salzburg offer numerous mountain biking trails, particularly around Untersberg and Gaisberg. These trails vary in difficulty, ensuring options for both beginners and experienced bikers.

3. Winter Sports

When winter arrives, Salzburg becomes a hub for skiing and snowboarding, attracting winter sports enthusiasts from all over. The nearby mountains offer a range of activities suitable for all skill levels.

3.1. Ski Resorts

- **Ski Amadé**: This is one of Austria's largest ski areas, with several resorts including Flachau, Wagrain, and Schladming. It features over 760 kilometers (472 miles) of slopes, making it an ideal destination for skiers and snowboarders.
- **Untersberg Ski Resort**: Located just outside Salzburg, Untersberg offers a local skiing experience with a variety of slopes suitable for different skill levels, making it a great option for families.
- **Dachstein Glacier**: For those wanting to ski in the summer, Dachstein Glacier offers year-round skiing opportunities. The glacier features various runs with stunning views of the surrounding mountains.

3.2. Other Winter Activities

- **Cross-Country Skiing**: The region boasts many well-marked cross-country skiing trails. Popular spots include Gaißau-Hintersee and the Fuschlsee area, perfect for those who prefer a leisurely pace while enjoying the winter scenery.
- **Snowshoeing**: Snowshoeing is a great way to explore the winter landscape at a slower pace. Many trails around Salzburg are suitable for snowshoeing, allowing you to experience the beauty of the snow-covered terrain.
- **Ice Skating**: In winter, many lakes freeze over, creating beautiful natural ice rinks. Popular spots for ice skating include Fuschlsee and Wolfgangsee lakes. There are also indoor ice rinks in Salzburg city for those who prefer to skate in a controlled environment.

4. Water Activities

With its proximity to beautiful lakes and rivers, Salzburg is a fantastic location for various water sports throughout the year.

4.1. Lakes

- **Lake Wolfgang**: Known for its stunning beauty, Lake Wolfgang is perfect for swimming, sailing, and paddleboarding. The lake features several beaches and swimming areas with facilities. In summer, you can rent pedal boats or take a cruise to enjoy the picturesque views.
- **Lake Fuschl**: This smaller lake is known for its clear waters and tranquil surroundings. Activities such as swimming, kayaking, and paddleboarding are popular here, and there are hiking trails around the lake.
- **Attersee Lake**: Attersee is one of the largest lakes in Austria, offering excellent conditions for sailing, windsurfing, and swimming. Several local schools provide courses for beginners interested in learning these water sports.

4.2. Rivers

- **Rafting**: The Salzach River and nearby rivers like the Saalach offer thrilling white-water rafting experiences. Various local companies organize guided rafting tours suitable for both beginners and experienced rafters, providing a fun way to enjoy the region's natural beauty.
- **Canoeing and Kayaking**: You can rent canoes or kayaks to explore the rivers and lakes at your leisure. Many rental shops offer guided tours for those who want to learn more about the local environment while enjoying their time on the water.

5. Wildlife Watching

Salzburg and its surroundings are rich in wildlife, making it an excellent place for nature lovers. The region is home to various animals, including deer, chamois, and numerous bird species.

5.1. Best Places for Wildlife Watching

- **National Park Hohe Tauern**: Austria's largest national park is home to a diverse range of wildlife. Guided tours are available, offering insights into the region's flora and fauna. Early morning or late afternoon hikes provide the best chances for spotting wildlife in their natural habitats.
- **Salzburger Lungau**: This area is known for its diverse ecosystems, making it a great place for animal spotting, including the majestic golden eagle. Many trails in the Lungau region are suitable for wildlife watching.
- **Untersberg Region**: This area is rich in animal life and offers excellent hiking trails for wildlife enthusiasts. The trails are well-marked, and early morning hikes provide the best chances to see animals in the wild.

6. Botanical Gardens and Parks

For those who prefer a more relaxed outdoor experience, Salzburg features beautiful parks and gardens where you can unwind and enjoy nature.

6.1. Mirabell Gardens

Located next to Mirabell Palace, the Mirabell Gardens are a stunning example of baroque landscape design. With beautifully arranged flowerbeds, fountains, and statues, it's a lovely place to take a leisurely stroll or enjoy a picnic while taking in views of the Hohensalzburg Fortress.

6.2. Salzburg Botanical Garden

The Salzburg Botanical Garden boasts a vast collection of plants from around the world. The garden features thematic sections, including a rock garden, tropical greenhouse, and herb garden. It's a peaceful spot for exploring and enjoying nature, with plenty of benches for resting.

6.3. Hellbrunn Palace Gardens

The gardens at Hellbrunn Palace are famous for their enchanting fountains and whimsical water features. These gardens provide a picturesque setting for leisurely walks, picnics, or simply enjoying the beauty of the outdoors.

7. Tips for Enjoying Outdoor Activities

- **Plan Ahead**: Before heading out, check the weather and trail conditions. Always carry a map or download offline maps to help navigate unfamiliar areas.

- **Dress Appropriately**: Wear comfortable, weather-appropriate clothing and sturdy shoes suitable for hiking or outdoor activities.
- **Stay Hydrated**: Bring enough water for your outdoor adventures, especially during warm summer days.
- **Respect Nature**: Follow local guidelines for wildlife watching and outdoor activities. Stick to marked trails and avoid disturbing the local flora and fauna.
- **Pack Snacks**: Bring along some snacks or a packed lunch to enjoy during your outdoor excursions. This way, you can take breaks and savor the beautiful surroundings.
- **Travel Off-Peak**: For a more peaceful experience, consider visiting popular trails and parks during weekdays or early mornings when crowds are fewer.

Travel Tips and Practical Information

8.1 Language and Communication

When traveling to Salzburg, understanding the local language and communication customs can greatly enhance your experience. Although many people in Salzburg speak English, especially in tourist areas, knowing a bit about the German language and local customs can help you connect with the culture and its people. This section provides an in-depth look at language and communication in Salzburg, offering tips to make your trip more enjoyable.

1. The Language of Salzburg

1.1. German Language Basics

The official language in Salzburg is German. The local dialect, known as "Salzburgerisch," is a variant of Austrian German, and while it may sound different from standard German, many speakers also understand High German. Here are some essential German phrases and words that can help you during your visit:

- **Hello** - Hallo
- **Goodbye** - Auf Wiedersehen
- **Please** - Bitte
- **Thank you** - Danke
- **Yes** - Ja
- **No** - Nein
- **Excuse me** - Entschuldigung
- **Do you speak English?** - Sprechen Sie Englisch?
- **How much does this cost?** - Wie viel kostet das?
- **Where is...?** - Wo ist...?
- **I don't understand.** - Ich verstehe nicht.

Learning these basic phrases can make interactions smoother and show locals that you respect their language and culture.

1.2. Local Dialects and Variations

In Salzburg, you may encounter various dialects, especially in rural areas. While most people will understand standard German, the local dialects may include unique words or phrases. Don't be afraid to ask locals to repeat themselves or clarify if you don't understand something.

2. English Proficiency

2.1. Understanding English in Salzburg

Many people in Salzburg, especially in the hospitality industry and tourist areas, speak English quite well. Young people and professionals in shops, hotels, and restaurants typically have a good command of English. You will likely find that menus, signs, and information brochures are available in English.

2.2. Tips for Communicating in English

While you can often get by speaking English, it's helpful to remember that some locals may not be fluent. Here are some tips for effective communication:

- **Speak Clearly**: Use simple words and clear sentences. Avoid speaking too fast, as this can make it harder for non-native speakers to understand.
- **Be Patient**: If someone is struggling to understand you, be patient and try rephrasing your question or statement.
- **Use Non-Verbal Communication**: Gestures, facial expressions, and body language can help convey your message if words fail.
- **Practice Your German**: If you know a few basic German phrases, use them! Locals appreciate the effort, and it can lead to friendlier interactions.

3. Cultural Communication Norms

Understanding cultural norms can enhance your communication and help you avoid misunderstandings. Here are some essential tips about communication customs in Salzburg:

3.1. Greetings and Introductions

- **Formal vs. Informal**: In Austria, it's common to use formal greetings when meeting someone for the first time. Address people as "Herr" (Mr.) or "Frau" (Mrs.) followed by their last name. If you become friends or have repeated encounters, you may switch to first names.
- **Handshake**: A firm handshake is the standard way to greet someone. Make eye contact and smile as you greet them, as this shows respect and friendliness.
- **Personal Space**: Austrians generally value personal space, so be mindful of how close you stand when talking to someone, especially if it's your first encounter.

3.2. Body Language

- **Gestures**: Different cultures have different meanings for gestures. In Austria, nodding typically means agreement, while shaking your head means disagreement.
- **Eye Contact**: Maintaining eye contact during conversation shows attentiveness and sincerity. However, too much direct eye contact can be perceived as aggressive, so find a comfortable balance.
- **Tipping**: Tipping is customary in restaurants and cafes. If you receive good service, it's common to round up the bill or leave around 5-10%.

4. Practical Tips for Communication

4.1. Mobile Phones and Internet Access

- **SIM Cards and Data Plans**: If you plan to stay in Salzburg for an extended period, consider purchasing a local SIM card to stay connected. Many shops, including those in the airport, offer prepaid SIM cards with data plans.
- **Wi-Fi Access**: Many cafes, restaurants, and hotels provide free Wi-Fi. When you enter a place, look for signs indicating Wi-Fi availability, or simply ask the staff for the password.

4.2. Translation Apps

Using translation apps can help bridge language gaps. Popular apps like Google Translate and Microsoft Translator can translate text and even voice conversations in real-time. Download these apps before your trip for easier communication.

4.3. Phrasebooks and Language Guides

Carrying a small phrasebook or language guide can be helpful, especially if you plan to visit areas where English may not be widely spoken. Look for books with practical phrases and cultural tips to enhance your experience.

5. Navigating Local Services

5.1. Asking for Help

When in need of assistance, it's common to ask locals for directions or recommendations. Here are a few phrases that can be useful:

- **Can you help me?** - Können Sie mir helfen?
- **Where is the nearest...?** - Wo ist die nächste...?
- **I'm looking for...** - Ich suche nach...

Most locals will be happy to help, even if they don't speak much English.

5.2. Communicating with Service Staff

In restaurants and shops, you may encounter staff with varying levels of English proficiency. Here are some tips for effective communication:

- **Order Simply**: When ordering food or drinks, keep it simple and clear. If a menu item has complex descriptions, ask the server for recommendations.
- **Specify Your Needs**: If you have dietary restrictions, allergies, or special requests, communicate them clearly. Use simple phrases like "I am allergic to…" (Ich bin allergisch gegen...) to ensure staff understand your needs.
- **Paying the Bill**: In many Austrian restaurants, it is customary to ask for the bill rather than waiting for it to be brought to you. Simply say, "Die Rechnung, bitte" (The bill, please).

6. Engaging with the Local Culture

6.1. Participating in Local Events

Salzburg hosts various events, concerts, and festivals throughout the year. Participating in these events is a great way to meet locals and practice your language skills. Here are some tips for engaging in local culture:

- **Ask About Events**: Inquire at your hotel or local information center about upcoming events. Use phrases like "Gibt es Veranstaltungen in der Nähe?" (Are there events nearby?).
- **Join Guided Tours**: Many tours are available in English, but you may also find tours offered in German. Joining a local tour can provide insights into the culture and history of the area.

6.2. Shopping and Souvenirs

When shopping in local markets or stores, you may want to ask for recommendations or inquire about products. Here are some helpful phrases:

- **What do you recommend?** - Was empfehlen Sie?
- **Is this handmade?** - Ist das handgemacht?
- **Can I try this on?** - Kann ich das anprobieren?

Local shopkeepers often appreciate customers who show interest in their products, even if you only know a few phrases in German.

7. Emergency Contacts and Assistance

7.1. Important Numbers

In case of emergencies, knowing key contact numbers is crucial. Here are important numbers to keep in mind:

- **Emergency Services (Police, Fire, Ambulance)**: 112
- **Local Police**: 133
- **Fire Department**: 122
- **Ambulance**: 144

It's also a good idea to have the contact information for your country's embassy or consulate in Austria.

7.2. Seeking Medical Assistance

If you need medical help, you can visit a local pharmacy (Apotheke) or hospital. Most pharmacies in Salzburg have staff who can communicate in English. If you need to explain your situation, try to stay calm and describe your symptoms clearly.

7.3. Using Emergency Services

In an emergency, dial 112 for assistance. The operator will ask for details about your situation. Stay as calm as possible, and provide information like your location and the nature of the emergency.

8. Building Connections

8.1. Making Friends

Connecting with locals can enhance your travel experience. Here are some tips for making friends while in Salzburg:

- **Attend Local Meetups**: Look for local groups or events on platforms like Meetup.com, where you can meet people with similar interests.
- **Participate in Classes**: Join classes or workshops that interest you, such as cooking or art classes. These settings often facilitate social interaction.
- **Engage in Conversations**: When you meet locals, express interest in their lives and culture. Simple questions about their favorite places to visit or local customs can lead to meaningful conversations.

9. Conclusion

Language and communication are essential aspects of any travel experience, and understanding the basics of German can greatly enhance your time in Salzburg. By learning a few key phrases, respecting local customs, and being open to engaging with locals, you'll create a richer and more enjoyable journey. Salzburg is not only a beautiful city but also a welcoming one, where the warmth of its people can make your visit truly memorable.

8.2 Currency and Payments

When traveling to Salzburg, understanding the currency and payment methods is essential for a smooth experience. This section covers everything you need to know about currency, how to make payments, and tips for managing your finances while exploring this beautiful Austrian city.

1. The Currency in Austria

1.1. Euro (€)

Austria uses the Euro as its official currency, represented by the symbol € and the code EUR. The Euro was introduced in Austria in 2002, replacing the Austrian Schilling. The Euro is used throughout the Eurozone, making it easy for travelers to use the same currency across many European countries.

1.2. Euro Coins and Banknotes

Euro currency comes in various denominations:

- **Coins**: €0.01, €0.02, €0.05, €0.10, €0.20, €0.50, €1, €2
- **Banknotes**: €5, €10, €20, €50, €100, €200, €500

When traveling, you'll frequently encounter €1 and €2 coins, which are useful for smaller purchases, such as public transportation fares or snacks.

2. Exchanging Currency

2.1. Currency Exchange Options

If you need to exchange your currency for Euros, several options are available:

- **Banks**: Most banks in Salzburg offer currency exchange services. They generally provide good rates, and you can withdraw cash from ATMs as well. Note that banks may charge a small fee for currency exchange.

- **Currency Exchange Offices**: Several currency exchange offices are located in the city center and near tourist attractions. While these places may offer convenient services, they may charge higher fees than banks.
- **Airports**: Currency exchange services are available at Salzburg Airport, but the rates may be less favorable compared to banks and local exchange offices. If possible, avoid exchanging large sums of money at the airport.

2.2. ATMs

ATMs are widely available throughout Salzburg, making it easy to withdraw cash as needed. Here are some tips for using ATMs:

- **International Fees**: Check with your bank regarding international withdrawal fees before your trip. Some banks offer cards that do not charge foreign transaction fees.
- **Choose Euros**: When using an ATM, you may be given the option to withdraw cash in your home currency. Always select the option to withdraw in Euros to avoid unfavorable exchange rates.
- **Security**: Use ATMs located in well-lit, busy areas, such as bank branches or shopping centers, to ensure your safety while withdrawing cash.

3. Payments in Salzburg

3.1. Cash vs. Card Payments

In Salzburg, both cash and card payments are widely accepted, but cash remains a popular choice, especially for smaller transactions. Here's what you need to know:

- **Cash Payments**: Many shops, cafes, and markets prefer cash payments. It's a good idea to carry some Euros for small purchases, such as pastries, souvenirs, or public transportation fares.
- **Card Payments**: Most hotels, restaurants, and larger stores accept credit and debit cards, especially Visa and MasterCard. American Express may be accepted in some places, but it's less common. Always check with the merchant if you're unsure whether they accept cards.
- **Contactless Payments**: Many establishments also accept contactless payment methods, such as Apple Pay or Google Pay. Ensure that your device is set up for international payments before your trip.

4. Tipping in Austria

Tipping is customary in Austria, but it's usually done in a relaxed manner compared to some other countries. Here's how tipping works in Salzburg:

4.1. Restaurants and Cafes

- **Service Charge**: In most restaurants, a service charge is included in the bill, but it's common to leave a small tip for good service. Rounding up the bill or adding about 5-10% is appreciated.
- **Cafes and Bars**: When ordering drinks or snacks at a cafe or bar, it's polite to leave small change. For example, if your bill is €4.50, you might give €5 and tell the server to keep the change.

4.2. Taxis

For taxi rides, it's customary to round up the fare or add a small tip (about 10%). If the driver helps with luggage, consider giving a little extra.

4.3. Hotels

In hotels, tipping is not mandatory, but you can give small amounts to staff for exceptional service. For example, you might tip housekeeping €1-2 per day or leave a tip for concierge services.

5. Managing Your Budget

5.1. Daily Expenses

Understanding the cost of living in Salzburg can help you plan your budget effectively. Here's an overview of typical daily expenses:

- **Meals**: A meal at an inexpensive restaurant may cost around €10-15, while a three-course meal for two at a mid-range restaurant may range from €50-70.
- **Public Transportation**: A single ticket for public transport costs around €2.80. If you plan to use public transport frequently, consider purchasing a day pass for around €7.40.
- **Attractions**: Entry fees for museums and attractions typically range from €10-15. Some places offer discounts for students, seniors, or families, so be sure to ask about any available deals.
- **Souvenirs**: Depending on what you buy, souvenirs can range from a few Euros for small items like postcards or magnets to €20-30 for more substantial gifts.

5.2. Creating a Budget

To help manage your finances while traveling, create a daily budget. Consider your planned activities, meals, and transportation costs, and set a reasonable limit. Keep track of your expenses to ensure you stay within your budget.

6. Emergency Cash Access

6.1. Emergency Funds

It's wise to have a backup plan for accessing cash in case of emergencies. Here are some suggestions:

- **Travel Money Cards**: Consider using a prepaid travel money card that you can load with Euros before your trip. These cards often come with lower fees than standard credit cards and provide a secure way to carry money.
- **Multiple Payment Methods**: Carry multiple payment methods, such as cash, a credit card, and a debit card. If one method fails or is lost, you'll have alternatives.

6.2. Emergency Contacts

Keep a record of your bank's contact information in case you need to report a lost or stolen card. Familiarize yourself with local ATM locations to ensure you can access cash when needed.

7. Conclusion

Understanding currency and payments in Salzburg is essential for a smooth travel experience. By familiarizing yourself with the Euro, payment methods, tipping customs, and budgeting tips, you can navigate your financial needs with ease. Being prepared allows you to enjoy all that this beautiful city has to offer without worrying about money. Whether you're dining at a cozy cafe, exploring local shops, or experiencing the rich culture, you'll be well-equipped to make the most of your trip to Salzburg.

8.3 Safety Tips and Emergency Contacts

Traveling to a new city can be both exciting and intimidating, especially when it comes to ensuring your safety. Salzburg, known for its stunning scenery, rich history, and vibrant culture, is generally a safe city for tourists. However, it's always wise to be prepared and informed. This section provides essential safety tips and important emergency contacts to help you have a safe and enjoyable trip to Salzburg.

1. General Safety Tips

1.1. Stay Aware of Your Surroundings

- **Stay Alert**: Always be aware of your surroundings, especially in crowded places like markets, tourist attractions, or public transportation. Watch out for pickpockets and keep your belongings secure.
- **Avoid Distractions**: When walking in busy areas, avoid distractions like using your phone or wearing headphones. Being aware of your surroundings can help you avoid potential dangers.

1.2. Keep Valuables Secure

- **Use a Money Belt**: Consider using a money belt or a hidden pouch for your cash, credit cards, and important documents. This makes it harder for thieves to access your valuables.
- **Lock Your Belongings**: If you're staying in a hostel or hotel, use a lock for your luggage and secure any valuables in a safe if available.

1.3. Stay in Well-Lit Areas

- **Avoid Dark Streets**: When exploring the city at night, stick to well-lit streets and busy areas. Avoid shortcuts through dark alleys or isolated parks, especially if you are alone.
- **Travel in Groups**: If possible, explore the city with friends or fellow travelers, especially at night. There's safety in numbers, and it can enhance your travel experience.

2. Emergency Contacts

2.1. Important Emergency Numbers

In case of emergencies, knowing the right numbers to call can make a significant difference. Here are some important emergency contacts in Salzburg:

- **Emergency Services (Police, Fire, Ambulance)**: Dial **112** for emergencies that require immediate assistance.
- **Local Police**: If you need to report a crime or require assistance, you can call **133**. The police can help with lost items, theft, or any other safety concerns.
- **Fire Department**: For fire emergencies, call **122**.
- **Ambulance**: If you require medical assistance, call **144**.

2.2. Non-Emergency Numbers

If you have a non-urgent situation or need information, here are some additional contacts:

- **Salzburg Tourist Information**: For general inquiries about the city, contact the tourist information center at **+43 662 8072 200**. They can provide you with information on attractions, accommodations, and local events.

- **Local Hospitals**: Familiarizing yourself with local hospitals can be beneficial in case of a medical emergency. Some hospitals in Salzburg include:
  - **Salzburg General Hospital (Universitätsklinikum Salzburg)**
    - Address: Müllerstraße 44, 5020 Salzburg
    - Phone: +43 662 21 80
  - **Private Hospital St. Joseph**
    - Address: Lehenstraße 11, 5020 Salzburg
    - Phone: +43 662 88 88 80

3. Health and Medical Tips

3.1. Health Insurance

Before traveling, ensure that you have adequate travel health insurance that covers medical emergencies while you are in Austria. Check your policy to know what is covered and how to contact your insurance provider in case of a medical emergency.

3.2. Carry a First Aid Kit

Bringing a small first aid kit can be helpful for minor injuries or illnesses. Include items like adhesive bandages, antiseptic wipes, pain relievers, and any personal medications you may need.

3.3. Know Basic Medical Terms

Familiarizing yourself with basic medical terminology in German can be beneficial in case you need medical assistance. Here are a few essential phrases:

- **I need a doctor** - Ich brauche einen Arzt.
- **Where is the nearest pharmacy?** - Wo ist die nächste Apotheke?
- **I'm allergic to...** - Ich bin allergisch gegen...

4. Personal Safety Measures

4.1. Be Cautious with Personal Information

When meeting new people or fellow travelers, be cautious about sharing personal information, such as your hotel details or travel plans. It's always wise to maintain some privacy.

4.2. Use Reputable Transportation

- **Public Transport**: Salzburg has an efficient public transportation system, including buses and trams. Stick to public transportation that is well-lit and busy, especially at night.

- **Taxis**: If you need to take a taxi, use reputable taxi companies or ride-sharing services like Uber, which may operate in the area.

4.3. Avoid Scams

While Salzburg is generally safe, be aware of common scams that may target tourists. Here are some tips to avoid scams:

- **Beware of Unofficial Guides**: If approached by someone offering guided tours or services on the street, be cautious. Always opt for licensed tour operators.
- **Keep an Eye on Your Belongings**: In crowded areas, be vigilant about your bags and belongings. If someone seems overly friendly or tries to engage you in conversation, keep your possessions close.

5. Natural Disaster Preparedness

While Salzburg is not prone to severe natural disasters, it's good to be aware of safety measures in case of emergencies:

5.1. Weather Awareness

- **Check the Weather**: Before heading out, check the weather forecast. In winter, be cautious of icy conditions, and in summer, stay hydrated and protected from the sun.
- **Emergency Weather Alerts**: Familiarize yourself with local emergency alerts regarding severe weather. These can usually be found on local news websites or through the Salzburg tourist office.

5.2. Earthquake Preparedness

While earthquakes are rare in Austria, it's still wise to be aware of basic safety measures in case of an earthquake:

- **Drop, Cover, and Hold On**: If you feel an earthquake, drop to the ground, take cover under a sturdy piece of furniture, and hold on until the shaking stops.
- **Know Evacuation Routes**: In your hotel, familiarize yourself with emergency exits and evacuation routes in case of a building emergency.

6. Conclusion

Safety is a crucial aspect of any travel experience, and being prepared can help ensure a smooth and enjoyable trip to Salzburg. By staying aware of your surroundings, knowing emergency contacts, and taking necessary precautions, you can focus on exploring the beauty of this city without worry. Remember, the locals in Salzburg are generally friendly and willing to help, so don't hesitate to reach out for assistance if needed. Enjoy your trip and create wonderful memories in this enchanting city!

8.4 Local Customs and Etiquette

Understanding local customs and etiquette is essential for a respectful and enjoyable travel experience. Salzburg, with its rich cultural heritage, has its own unique traditions and social norms. This section provides insights into local customs, dining etiquette, and appropriate behavior to help you navigate social situations while in Salzburg.

1. Greetings and Social Interactions

1.1. Common Greetings

In Austria, greetings are an important part of social interaction. Here are some common ways to greet people:

- **Hallo**: This is a casual greeting, similar to "Hello." It can be used in most situations.
- **Guten Tag**: This means "Good day" and is a more formal greeting suitable for use in shops, restaurants, and with acquaintances.
- **Grüß Gott**: A traditional Bavarian greeting, it translates to "God greet you." It is commonly used in Salzburg and other regions of Austria, especially in rural areas.
- **Tschüss**: This is a casual way to say goodbye.

When meeting someone, it is customary to make eye contact, smile, and offer a firm handshake. If you are greeting friends or acquaintances, a light kiss on the cheek (usually once on each cheek) is common among women and between women and men.

1.2. Personal Space

Austrians typically value personal space, so it's important to be mindful of this during conversations. Avoid standing too close to someone you don't know well, as this may make them feel uncomfortable.

2. Dining Etiquette

Dining customs in Salzburg reflect the region's traditions and respect for food. Here are some key points to keep in mind when dining out:

2.1. Table Manners

- **Wait to be Seated**: In restaurants, wait to be seated by a host or hostess. If you're in a more casual place, feel free to choose your table.
- **Keep Your Hands on the Table**: During meals, it is polite to keep your hands on the table (but not your elbows). This shows attentiveness and engagement in the dining experience.
- **Use Cutlery Properly**: Use your knife and fork for eating; it's considered impolite to eat with your fingers, except for certain foods like bread.
- **Finish Your Plate**: While it's not mandatory, it is often appreciated if you finish your meal. Leaving food on your plate may be seen as wasteful.

2.2. Toasting

If you're dining with others and drinks are served, it is customary to offer a toast before starting your meal. A common toast in Austria is **"Prost!"** (Cheers!). Make sure to maintain eye contact when clinking glasses, as this is seen as a sign of respect.

3. Dress Code

3.1. Dressing Appropriately

Austria has a relatively formal dress code compared to some other countries. When visiting restaurants, theaters, or churches, it's advisable to dress neatly. Here are some tips:

- **Casual Wear**: Casual clothing is acceptable in most situations, but avoid overly casual attire like sweatpants or beachwear when dining out.
- **Church Visits**: When visiting churches, including Salzburg Cathedral, dress modestly. It's common to cover shoulders and knees.
- **Seasonal Considerations**: Be prepared for the weather, especially if you're visiting during winter when warm clothing is essential. Comfortable walking shoes are also recommended for exploring the city.

4. Tipping Practices

Tipping in Austria is customary, and it's important to know how much to tip and when:

4.1. Restaurant Tipping

- **Service Included**: Most restaurants include a service charge in the bill, but it's common to leave a small tip (around 5-10% of the total bill) for good service.
- **Rounding Up**: If you prefer not to calculate percentages, rounding up to the nearest Euro is a common practice. For example, if your bill is €18, you could leave €20 and tell the server to keep the change.

4.2. Tipping in Taxis and Cafés

- **Taxis**: It's customary to round up the fare or add a small tip (about 10%) for taxi drivers, especially if they assist with your luggage.
- **Cafés and Bars**: In casual settings, leaving small change is appreciated. If your coffee costs €2.50, handing over €3 and asking to keep the change is common.

5. Festivals and Traditions

Salzburg has a rich tradition of festivals and cultural events that reflect its history and customs. Being aware of local celebrations can enhance your experience:

5.1. Advent Season and Christmas Markets

The holiday season in Salzburg is particularly magical, with Christmas markets filling the city with lights and festive cheer. If you're visiting during this time, partake in the local customs:

- **Advent**: The four weeks leading up to Christmas are celebrated with Advent wreaths, candles, and traditional music. It's customary to enjoy seasonal treats, such as **Lebkuchen** (gingerbread) and **Glühwein** .
- **Christmas Markets**: Attend local Christmas markets, where you can buy handmade crafts, decorations, and traditional food. It's polite to browse and engage with vendors while enjoying the festive atmosphere.

5.2. Music Festivals

Salzburg is renowned for its musical heritage, especially for being the birthplace of Wolfgang Amadeus Mozart. If you have the chance to attend music festivals, be sure to:

- **Respect Performances**: Maintain silence during performances and refrain from using your phone. Applauding at the appropriate moments is appreciated.
- **Dress Appropriately**: For concerts and operas, dress smartly. Many attendees wear formal or semi-formal attire.

6. Respecting Local Customs

6.1. Respecting Quiet Hours

In Austria, quiet hours are typically observed between 10 PM and 6 AM, especially in residential areas. This means loud noises, such as music or parties, should be minimized during these hours. Be considerate of your neighbors, whether in hotels or residential areas.

6.2. Environmental Awareness

Austrians are generally environmentally conscious. When traveling in Salzburg, follow local customs regarding waste disposal and recycling. Make sure to separate your waste and use designated recycling bins.

7. Conclusion

Being aware of local customs and etiquette in Salzburg will enhance your travel experience and help you connect with the culture. By respecting greetings, dining practices, and social norms, you'll be able to navigate social situations confidently and create positive interactions with locals. Embrace the traditions and warmth of Salzburg, and enjoy your journey in this beautiful city!

Conclusion

Salzburg is a city that seamlessly blends history, culture, and natural beauty, creating an enchanting experience for travelers. As the birthplace of Wolfgang Amadeus Mozart and the backdrop for the beloved musical "The Sound of Music," Salzburg has a unique charm that attracts visitors from around the world. From its stunning architecture and vibrant music scene to its rich culinary traditions and warm, welcoming locals, there's much to discover and experience.

As you navigate through the charming streets lined with baroque buildings, take a moment to appreciate the city's architectural splendor. The iconic **Hohensalzburg Fortress**, perched atop the Mönchsberg mountain, offers panoramic views of the city and surrounding Alps. This impressive fortress is not just a historical landmark; it is a testament to Salzburg's rich past and its significance in European history. A visit here is a must, as it allows you to step back in time and understand the strategic importance of this region.

Exploring the old town, a UNESCO World Heritage Site, you'll encounter narrow alleys, quaint shops, and bustling squares, each with its own story to tell. The **Getreidegasse**, a famous shopping street, showcases the city's rich mercantile history and is also home to Mozart's Birthplace. This vibrant area is not only a shopper's paradise but also a cultural hub, brimming with cafes, artisan shops, and local markets.

Immerse Yourself in Local Culture

To truly appreciate Salzburg, you must immerse yourself in the local customs and etiquette. Whether you're savoring traditional dishes, enjoying the picturesque scenery, or engaging with friendly residents, being respectful and open-minded will enhance your journey. The locals take pride in their culture, and showing interest in their traditions can lead to enriching conversations and experiences.

Salzburg's culinary scene is a reflection of its history and geographical location. Do not miss the chance to try local specialties like **Sachertorte**, a decadent chocolate cake, and **Salzburger Nockerl**, a fluffy dessert that is as delightful to eat as it is to look at. Dining in one of Salzburg's traditional restaurants or taverns is not just about the food; it's about the experience. Engage with your servers and ask for recommendations—many are eager to share their favorites and stories about the dishes.

Additionally, attending local festivals or music events can provide a deeper understanding of Salzburg's cultural heartbeat. The city hosts numerous events throughout the year, celebrating everything from classical music to Christmas markets filled with crafts and local delicacies. Participating in these festivities allows you to connect with the local community and experience their traditions firsthand.

Planning Your Visit

In planning your visit, keep in mind the importance of preparation. Understanding transportation options, accommodation choices, and safety measures will ensure a smooth experience. Salzburg is well-connected by public transport, making it easy to explore not only the city but also the stunning surrounding areas. Buses and trams are efficient and convenient, allowing you to visit attractions without the hassle of parking or navigating through traffic.

Consider investing in a Salzburg Card, which offers free access to public transportation and discounts on many attractions. This card is particularly useful for first-time visitors, as it simplifies your travel plans and allows for spontaneous exploration without the worry of additional costs.

Accommodation in Salzburg ranges from luxurious hotels to charming hostels, catering to all budgets. When selecting where to stay, consider your preferences for location and amenities. Staying in the old town provides easy access to major attractions, while neighborhoods slightly outside the city center may offer a quieter atmosphere and often better rates. Researching options online and reading reviews can help you find a place that meets your needs.

Always be aware of your surroundings, especially in crowded tourist areas. While Salzburg is generally a safe city, it's wise to stay vigilant and keep your belongings secure. Make sure to have a plan for unexpected situations, such as locating emergency services or understanding local health facilities in case of illness. Having a basic understanding of local customs and emergency numbers can also enhance your peace of mind while traveling.

Discovering Salzburg's Stories

From the enchanting **Hohensalzburg Fortress** to the beautiful **Mirabell Gardens** and the musical legacy of Mozart, every corner of Salzburg holds a story waiting to be discovered. The gardens, designed in the 18th century, are not only a beautiful sight but also a symbol of Salzburg's artistic heritage. Strolling through these gardens, you can enjoy meticulously maintained flower beds, impressive fountains, and stunning views of the fortress. It's a perfect spot for a leisurely afternoon or a romantic evening walk.

Don't forget to visit the **Salzburg Cathedral**, a magnificent baroque structure that stands as a testament to the city's religious heritage. The cathedral's stunning interior and impressive dome are worth the visit alone, and attending a service or concert can provide an unforgettable experience. This sacred space has witnessed centuries of history and remains a focal point for both locals and visitors alike.

As you prepare for your trip, pack your enthusiasm and curiosity. Be open to new experiences and willing to explore beyond the typical tourist paths. Consider taking a guided walking tour to learn more about Salzburg's hidden gems and historical significance. Engaging with knowledgeable guides can provide unique insights and help you uncover aspects of the city you might not discover on your own.

Creating Lasting Memories

Salzburg welcomes you with open arms, offering a rich tapestry of experiences that will stay with you long after your visit. Take time to relax and soak in the stunning landscapes, whether you're enjoying the view from the fortress or wandering through the countryside. The surrounding regions, such as the **Salzkammergut Lake District**, are perfect for day trips and outdoor adventures. Here, you can hike, cycle, or simply bask in the natural beauty of Austria.

Consider capturing your memories through photography or journaling about your experiences. Reflecting on your adventures will allow you to savor the moments long after you've returned home. Share your stories with friends and family, inspiring them to explore Salzburg and the rich culture it offers.

As you journey through this beautiful city, remember that travel is about more than just the sights—it's about the connections you make, the experiences you share, and the stories you gather along the way. Engage with locals, embrace new traditions, and open yourself to the unexpected.

Final Thoughts

In conclusion, Salzburg is a city that captivates the heart and soul of its visitors. Its blend of history, culture, and stunning landscapes creates an unforgettable experience. By immersing yourself in local customs, exploring its attractions, and engaging with the community, you can create a meaningful connection with this remarkable city.

May your journey to Salzburg be filled with delightful moments, enriching encounters, and lasting memories. Enjoy your time in this beautiful city, and may your travels lead you to new adventures and discoveries in the future. Safe travels, and may you return home with a heart full of stories and a spirit enriched by your experiences in Salzburg!

Acknowledgments

Creating this travel guide to Salzburg has been a rewarding journey, and I would like to take a moment to express my gratitude to those who have contributed to its development.

First and foremost, a heartfelt thank you to the residents of Salzburg for their warmth and hospitality. Their kindness and willingness to share their knowledge about their city have enriched this guide immeasurably. The insights gained from locals about customs, traditions, and hidden gems have provided a deeper understanding of what makes Salzburg a unique destination.

I also extend my appreciation to travel enthusiasts and bloggers who have shared their experiences and tips online. Their stories and recommendations have been invaluable in shaping the information presented in this guide. The travel community's collaborative spirit fosters a wealth of knowledge that benefits all who seek to explore new places.

Special thanks go to the tourism boards and local organizations dedicated to preserving Salzburg's cultural heritage. Their efforts in promoting the city's attractions, events, and history have made it easier for travelers to appreciate all that Salzburg has to offer.

I would also like to acknowledge the friends and family who have supported this project, providing feedback and encouragement throughout the writing process. Their enthusiasm for travel and exploration has inspired me to create a guide that is both informative and engaging.

Lastly, a sincere thank you to the readers. Your interest in discovering Salzburg inspires the continued exploration of our world's diverse cultures and histories. I hope this guide serves as a helpful companion on your journey, leading you to unforgettable experiences in this enchanting city.

Printed in Great Britain
by Amazon